WEAPON

THE UZI
SUBMACHINE GUN

CHRIS McNAB

Series Editor Martin Pegler

First published in Great Britain in 2011 by Osprey Publishing,
Midland House, West Way, Botley, Oxford, OX2 0PH, UK
44-02 23rd Street, Suite 219, Long Island City, NY 11101, USA

E-mail: info@ospreypublishing.com

A CIP catalogue record for this book is available from the
British Library

Print ISBN: 978 1 84908 543 4

PDF ebook ISBN: 978 1 84908 544 1

ePub ebook ISBN: 978 1 84908 906 7

Page layout by Mark Holt

Battlescene artwork by Johnny Shumate

Exploded diagram by Alan Gilliland

Index by Alan Thatcher

Typeset in Sabon and Univers

Originated by Blenheim Colour

Printed in China through Worldprint

11 12 13 14 15   10 9 8 7 6 5 4 3 2 1

Osprey Publishing is supporting the Woodland Trust, the UK's
leading woodland conservation charity, by funding the dedication
of trees.

Cover images are courtesy of Israel Weapon Industries (top) and
the US Air Force (bottom).

Acknowledgements

Several people have made an important contribution to the
production of this book. First and foremost, I would like to
thank Amihai Dekel of Israel Weapon Industries (IWI), for
his frequent and friendly support in providing information,
documents and photographs for this title, and helping correct
some of my misperceptions. Without his assistance, writing
this book would have been a more complicated affair. I would
also like to thank Nick Reynolds of Osprey for his professional
management of the project, and Ted Nevill of Cody Images
for finding more good photographs. I am further grateful to
Johnny Shumate and Alan Gilliland, for the superb artworks
here. Finally, the 'Uzitalk' forum (<www.uzitalk.com>) has been
a useful resource for finding out more about the Uzi and those
who use it.

Editor's note

The following will help in converting measurements between
imperial and metric:

1 mile = 1.6km
1 yard = 0.9m
1ft = 0.3m
1in = 2.54cm/25.4mm

CONTENTS

INTRODUCTION

The Uzi submachine gun (SMG) surely ranks alongside the AK-47 as perhaps history's most recognizable firearm. Its fame, as these pages shall explore, is entirely warranted. Few firearms have brought together sheer firepower and compact dimensions so successfully as the Uzi. Its close-range lethality, and distribution figures in their millions, have ensured its popularity across the full spectrum of possible users. Throughout its lifespan to date Uzis have been seen in the hands of infantrymen, armoured vehicle crews, special forces soldiers, law-enforcement officers, Secret Service agents, civilian enthusiasts, Hollywood stars and outright criminals. Almost all without exception developed an enormous respect for the weapon, both for its ability to save life – their own – and its capacity for killing.

To understand the Uzi fully, as well as its status in post-1945 history, it needs to be placed in its long-term context. In 1914, the world submerged itself in the greatest conflict since the Napoleonic Wars. Millions of men mobilized for war, and found themselves deployed far from home on nameless battlefields, there to kill, survive or die. For almost all of these men, the personal weapon with which they fought was the bolt-action rifle. Such firearms had an ancestry stretching back to the first half of the 19th century, with the development of the breech-loading unitary cartridge and the forerunner of all bolt-action rifles, the 'Needle Gun' designed by Prussian gunsmith Johann Nikolaus von Dreyse (1787–1867). Refinements in the second half of the 19th century by the likes of Antoine Chassepot (1833–1905), the Mauser brothers Paul (1838–1914) and Wilhelm (1834–82), and James Paris Lee (1831–1904) led to the perfection of the bolt-action design, and its standardization within the world's armies. In weapons like the 7.92mm Mauser Gewehr 98, the .303in Short Magazine Lee-Enfield (SMLE) and the .30-06 Springfield, soldiers had firearms that were tough, powerful and foolproof to use.

Bolt-action rifles would serve soldiers well until the end of World War II, but the first global war of the 20th century did highlight a problem with the type. World War I, at least on the Western Front, stagnated into trench warfare, and for trench assaults the bolt-action rifle proved to be of questionable merit. For a start, such rifles were long and unwieldy in the confines of a trench or in urban combat – the Mauser Gewehr 98 of the German Army, for example, measured 1,255mm (over 4ft), hardly convenient for taking snap-shots in a bunker doorway, or in a narrow communications trench. Furthermore, in close-range fighting, the bolt-action was a worryingly slow reloading mechanism. Firing a shot every two seconds or so might have been fine from your own lines, but at close quarters, with threats popping up thick and fast, each period of bolt operation left the user exposed. Compounding the problem was the fact that the typical magazine capacity of the bolt-action rifle was low – the SMLE had a ten-shot magazine, and this was well stacked compared to many other models.

The final issue with the bolt-action rifle – a problem that would also lead to the invention of the assault rifle – was that its cartridge was simply too powerful for realistic combat. The Lee-Enfield's cartridge, which had similar characteristics to those of many contemporary rifles, delivered a 174-grain bullet at a muzzle velocity of 617m/sec, giving a lethal range in excess of a mile. This was all well and good for long-range shooting, but at close ranges the bullet was unnecessarily muscular, liable to cut straight through the opponent and continue onwards. Recoil was also hefty, reducing the accuracy of shots when taken frequently.

What was needed, at least for those troops engaged in close-range assaults, was a different type of weapon – smaller, lighter, quicker to reload, and with greater firepower within ranges of about 100m. By World War I, automatic firepower was already on the battlefield in the form of machine guns like the German MG 08 and British Vickers, but even the light machine gun (LMG) varieties such as the Lewis gun still fired the .303in British rifle round and needed to be at least bipod-mounted to fire effectively.

IDF troops attack the Jordanian-controlled West Bank village of Samua, 1960s. Three soldiers are armed with Uzis (the soldier in the centre is reloading), while their prone comrade has a heavy-barrelled FN FAL rifle for light support. The 7.62mm FAL was one of the last successful full-bore battle rifles; after World War II, pistol-calibre submachine guns like the Uzi and intermediate-calibre assault rifles became increasingly dominant. (Cody Images)

In 1915, a weapon appeared that had the potential to fill the 'firepower gap'. This was the Italian Villar-Perosa. At first glance, the weapon looks like a rather odd LMG. It had two barrels and actions, a bipod and spade grips (it could also be fitted with a tripod and shield), and each action took a curved 25-round detachable box magazine. Yet here in many ways was history's first SMG. Instead of a rifle cartridge, it fired the 9×19mm Glisenti pistol round (this actually had the same dimensions as the future 9×19mm Parabellum, but with reduced power), developing a muzzle velocity of 365m/sec, around half that of contemporary rifle bullets. It operated via a delayed-blowback system. Blowback meant that just the mass of the bolt and the force of the return spring held the cartridge in place at the moment of firing – the limited recoil force of the pistol cartridge meant that positive bolt locking was not required. The delay part of the operation, which served to ensure firing pressures had dropped to safe levels before the bolt opened, was delivered by a lug riding through a 15-degree angle in a groove in the receiver wall (the striker also had a cam and groove arrangement within the bolt). The rearward force of the cartridge had to turn the bolt before the bolt opened and ejection and reloading occurred.

The technicalities of the Villar-Perosa were doubtless lost on most Italian soldiers who took the weapon into action in 1915, but its capabilities were not. It could fire, with manageable recoil and decent accuracy over 100m or so, at a blistering rate of 1,200rpm.

The combination of blowback operation, a pistol round and fast full-auto fire makes the Villar-Perosa effectively the first SMG in history. Yet its bulky, two-barrel design compromised its utility and few were made, so the honour of ushering in the age of truly practical SMGs went to a German weapon, the Bergmann MP 18. Around 1916 German general Oskar von Hutier (1857–1934), an innovator in infantry tactics, looked for a new weapon suited to use by light, fast assault teams of 'Stormtroopers'. Hugo Schmeisser, the chief designer for the Theodor Bergmann company, responded by producing a single-barrel pure blowback weapon, firing what

Where the SMG journey started. The 9mm Villar-Perosa looked in many ways like a light machine gun, but its pistol-calibre round and blowback action made it an SMG in principle. (Cody Images)

The 9×19mm Parabellum cartridge

Round length:	29.98mm
Case length:	19.35mm
Rim diameter:	9.94mm
Bullet weight:	7.45g (115 grains)
Length of bullet:	15.7mm
Weight of powder charge:	0.4g (6.2 grains)
Muzzle velocity:	*c.* 400m/sec

has become a staple round for most SMGs to this day – the 9×19mm Parabellum. At first the MP 18, as it was known, fired from a 32-round helical drum magazine, but this was eventually discarded in favour of a 20- or 32-round straight box magazine. Firing rate was 500rpm.

The MP 18 came late in the war, so only 36,000 were made. Yet the weapon was solidly made for battlefield use, and delivered devastating power at close ranges, although these characteristics were only proven in a few localized battles. The SMG was not designed to replace the bolt-action rifle – long-range, powerful fire was still required, and the bolt-action had great virtues of simplicity for conscript armies – but it could serve as a valued part of the squad, platoon and company firepower. The concept of the SMG had been proven.

Between the creation of the MP 18 and the Uzi SMG in the late 1940s, the world's armies bought enthusiastically into the principles of pistol-calibre automatic firepower. World War II saw every army carry SMG types into battle – landmark weapons such as the British Sten, the US Thompson and M3, the German MP 38 and MP 40 and the Soviet PPSh 41. To meet wartime production needs, such guns were frequently crude tributes to the processes of welding and steel stamping, utilizing the most basic of blowback systems and rudimentary manufacturing processes. They showed, however, the value of manportable automatic firepower, particularly in a war of assault and manoeuvre. This would be realized three decades later, when one Uziel Gal looked to create a new weapon for the Israeli armed services.

DEVELOPMENT
Uziel Gal's invention

On 14 May 1948, the State of Israel declared itself independent, born from the troubled rule of the British Mandate of Palestine. While a moment of genuine pride for Israel's leaders and people, independence was also a time of threat. Fighting between the Jewish people and regional Arabs had been swelling from the beginning of the 20th century, particularly since the Balfour Declaration of 1917 declared Britain to be in favour of the 'establishment in Palestine of a national home for the Jewish people'. Jewish fighters organized themselves into improvised but organized military bodies, eventually giving rise to the Hagana militia of the 1930s. The Hagana, its elite sub-group known as the Palmach (established 1941), and other Jewish armed groups received invaluable military training and combat experience alongside the British during World War II. The resulting professionalization was then put to work against new enemies, fighting both Arabs and British in the immediate post-war period. This insurgency campaign brought the ultimate reward – the May 1948 declaration that established Israel as a nation-state. By the end of the month, Hagana and the other militias had transformed themselves into the Israel Defense Forces (IDF).

There was scarcely a moment to rejoice. Within hours of independence, Israel was attacked by the combined forces of Egypt, Trans-Jordan, Syria and Lebanon, which despite their overwhelming superiority in manpower and firepower, were roundly defeated by an ingenious and determined Israeli defence. Yet even with the Israeli victory, the fact remained that the IDF was operating on a shoestring using a motley arsenal of war surplus and home-produced weapons of uncertain quality, and with no standardization amongst or across units. That situation was particularly pronounced in terms of small arms. To fight the War of Independence,

Israeli troops gathered some 200 machine guns, 10,000 rifles and 3,600 SMGs from whatever sources they could – arms dumps left over in North Africa from World War II; trade with disgruntled British soldiers; user-dangerous home-made types; even supplies from Arab dealers. The guns in use included SMLE and Mauser Kar 98k rifles, British Sten guns and German MP 40s, civilian hunting rifles and shotguns. In firearms historian Ian Hogg's words: 'The result of all this was a motley collection of weapons of every type and vintage, demanding a wide range of ammunition, which would, in a properly-organized army, have led to a logistical nightmare of supply problems'.[1] If the IDF was to sculpt itself into a proper army, this situation had to change – it needed new weapons.

Israeli infantry assaulting Egyptian forces in the Negev area of Israel during the 1948 War of Independence. At independence the IDF was equipped with a mixture of war surplus, home-made and commercially purchased small arms. (Keystone/Getty Images)

THE BIRTH OF THE UZI

Uziel Gal (1923–2002) was born on 15 December 1923 in Weimar, Germany, and was originally named Gothard Glas, the son of Erich and Miele Glas. Ten years after Gothard's birth, Adolf Hitler came to power in Germany, and the country's Jews began to experience the growing horror of Nazi persecution. The young Gothard was fortunate, in a roundabout way. His parents divorced when he was still young, and in 1933 Gothard went to live in Britain for a while, having moved there with his Jewish school. His father, however, had emigrated to Palestine, and there Gothard moved in 1936. He settled in the northern part of the country and took his family's new Hebrew name, Gal.

[1] Hogg, *Israeli War Machine*, p.15

Apparently, Gal showed an interest in firearms design throughout his teenage years, demonstrated by his creation of an automatic arrow-thrower at the age of 15. A military career beckoned, and following his graduation from the Kibbutz Yagur he joined the Palmach as a weapons engineer. Imprisoned by the British for two years from 1943, having been caught carrying a gun (his sentence was actually for six years), Gal went into the IDF on independence, fighting in the 1948 war and training as an officer.

Now the weapon that would eventually bear his name enters the picture in earnest. In the late 1940s, the major arms producer in Israel was Israel Military Industries (IMI), formed as an underground organization in 1933. With independence, IMI became the official state arms manufacturer, a part of the Ministry of Defense. In 1948, dissatisfied at the state of its small-arms inventory, IMI commissioned two firearms engineers to produce designs for a decent individual weapon for Israel soldiers, principally to replace the rough and ready Sten guns in the system. These designers, both IDF officers, were Lieutenant Uziel Gal and Major Chaim Kara, the latter head of the light weapons section in the IDF Ordnance Corps. Gal had already come to IMI's attention when, while he was undergoing officer training, he had demonstrated a new model of SMG he was designing. On the basis of this model, he was employed by IMI. The outcome of the design competition between him and Kara would be ruthlessly judged on merit, and both now set themselves to designing the perfect SMG.

Neither engineer was working in a vacuum, and in the case of Gal there was clear inspiration. In the late 1940s, the Czech firearms manufacturer Ceskoslovenska Zbrojovka (CZ) began production of an innovative series of blowback SMGs, the CZ (or Samopal – Sa.) 23, 24, 25 and 26, designed primarily by one Vaclav Holecek. Two features in particular distinguished the CZ SMGs. First, the magazine inserted directly into the pistol grip,

rather than sitting in a separate housing in front of the trigger guard. This positioning was enabled by virtue of the gun's second critical feature, a telescoping bolt. In this design, the front section of the bolt was tubular, and wrapped around the rear end of the barrel when chambering and firing the cartridge. The value of this design was that it retained the appropriate bolt mass to control the rearward forces of blowback operation, but the tubular design meant that the overall length of the gun could be reduced.

Thousands of the CZ series SMGs were exported to the Middle East, including Israel, where they provided inspiration to Gal and Kara as they battled to give the IDF its new weapon. In the early 1950s, both men submitted weapons to competitive trials. Kara's contribution was the 9mm Kara Model K-12. Like the CZ firearms, the K-12 was a blowback, telescoping bolt design, feeding from a 20- or 40-round magazine inserted

The early versions of the Uzi came with a wooden stock, which could be removed if desired. The stock could also hold a cleaning rod and a bottle of gun oil behind the butt plate. (Cody Images)

A key influence on the design of the Uzi was the weapon seen here, the Czech CZ 25. As we can see, it incorporated the pistol-grip housing for the magazine and a folding stock, and it also utilized a telescoping bolt. (Cody Images)

An Uzi issued to the Dutch Army during the 1980s. The colouration around the muzzle possibly indicates that it is a training weapon. The Netherlands was the first country after Israel to order the Uzi for its armed forces. (Cody Images)

into the pistol grip (although Kara's early prototypes were of conventional front-magazine layout). It was a decent gun – easy to fire and strip, and made with high-quality manufacturing processes. Ironically, here was its problem. For a young nation with an emerging economy, the K-12 looked an expensive option. Gal's contribution, however, worked along the same general principles but its design was based on cheaper and quicker stamped metal construction, and it avoided the fine tolerances of the K-12, which made it more rugged for field use. It also had 12 fewer parts than the K-12, further reducing costs.

In 1951, a total of 12 K-12s and five 'Uzis' were put through trials, testing out their endurance and performance in the grinding conditions of the desert. Taking into account all factors, the Uzi was the clear winner and it was selected for further development. In an interesting aside, Gal was actually resistant to the idea of his name being modified for use as the gun's title – he was evidently overridden. Gal patented the weapon in 1952, although with production rights granted to the Israeli Ministry of Defense, and the Uzi went through further trials and field testing. Eventually, in March 1954, the Ordnance Corps placed an order for 8,000 Uzis and 80,000 magazines. The Uzi was now in service.

DESIGN OF THE UZI

Internal mechanism

The Uzi offered a revolutionary package to the front-line soldier. It was easy to fire and control, even though it could spew out 9×19mm Parabellum cartridges at a cyclical rate of 600rpm. By locating the magazine in the pistol grip, the centre of gravity sat neatly and directly in the hand, even allowing for controllable one-handed firing. The magazine location also had the advantage of intuitive reloading in night-time conditions or under the stresses of combat – the soldier simply had to remember the 'hand-finds-hand' principle. An Uzi could be field stripped in seconds, and by having only a small number of parts the gun was less fiddly to maintain in the field, with a reduced chance of losing an integral item.

Looking at the design in more detail, the Uzi is, as already noted, a blowback weapon with a telescoping breech-block. The original, standard Uzi is an open-bolt gun, meaning that once the gun is loaded and cocked, the breech-block is held to the rear position by the trigger sear. When the trigger is pulled, the sear releases the breech-block, which drives forward under the power of the return spring. As it moves, the lower edge of the breech-block catches the uppermost cartridge in the magazine stack, pushing against the top edge of the cartridge base. The breech-block continues onwards now with the cartridge, and as it does so the cartridge contacts a feed ramp, which lifts it upwards slightly to guide it into the mouth of the chamber, at the same time stripping the cartridge clear of the magazine. Completing its travel, the breech-block now comes to a stop at the mouth of the chamber, the tubular part wrapping around the rear section of the barrel. Note that at this moment the extractors rise and the base of the cartridge moves into a recess in the breech-block, which holds the firing pin. As the breech-block comes to a stop, the firing pin strikes the percussion cap in the base of the cartridge and the weapon fires.

Like the original Uzi, this Mini Uzi has an open-bolt configuration. We can also see the simplicity of the barrel mounting, secured in place by a large barrel retaining nut, seen on the far left of this view. The Mini Uzi, introduced in 1980, was also offered as a closed-bolt model. (Israel Weapon Industries)

Half of the Uzi's action is now complete; the gun now needs to extract and eject the empty case and reload. The pressures of cartridge ignition create recoil and a rearward pressure on the breech-block, whose mass keeps the empty case in situ until the bullet has left the barrel and the pressures have dropped to safe levels. Then the breech-block starts its rearward journey against the tension of the return spring. At the same time, an extractor claw grips the base rim of the spent case, keeping the case in the breech-block until it is level with the rear face of the ejection port, on the right-hand side of the receiver. At this point an ejector mechanism strikes the base of the cartridge, pivoting it around the extractor and pushing the case out through the ejection port. (Note that as the breech-block moves past the magazine, the magazine spring pushes up the stack of rounds to present a new cartridge ready for firing.)

The breech-block continues backwards in the Uzi until it comes to the rear of the receiver, the return spring having built up considerable pressure. The spring then drives the breech-block back forward. One of two things now happens. The Uzi has three fire modes, controlled by a sliding selector switch on the left side of the weapon, at the top of the pistol grip. It has three settings – A, R and S – denoted on a scale above the selector switch: A = 'Automatic' (full-auto fire, i.e. continuous fire with a single trigger pull); R = 'Repetition' (semi-auto fire, i.e. one shot fired with each trigger pull); S = 'Safety' (unable to fire). If the selector is set to A, the breech-block makes a full journey forward to strip and fire another cartridge; the cycle will continue as long as the trigger is held down. If the selector is set to R, the sear in the trigger engages the breech-block and holds it in the rear position, only to be released with another pull of the trigger.

From the ground up, the Uzi was built to be rigorously safe, and all variants have three levels of safety mechanism. The 'S' setting on the selector switch prevents the trigger from being depressed in conventional fashion, but at the back of the pistol grip is also a grip safety mechanism. This has to be squeezed in by the action of gripping the pistol grip before the gun will fire, protecting against discharges if the gun is knocked or

The selector switch and the pistol grip of Uzi weapons follow a common format (although the letters above the selector can change depending on the country). Note the grip safety feature on the back of the pistol grip. (Israel Weapon Industries)

dropped. A final level of safety is provided by a ratcheting safety feature on the cocking mechanism, which prevents the gun from firing if the bolt is released accidentally during the cocking procedure.

External features

Moving from the internal to the external parts of the Uzi, the first generation of Uzis were fitted with solid, quick-detachable wooden stocks, fitted to the gun via an I-shaped bracket. Note that some of these early stocks came with apertures drilled into them for holding a cleaning rod and an oil bottle. In total, about four varieties of the wooden stock were produced, each with slightly different dimensions and profiles.

A critical change in stock configuration for the Uzi came in 1967, when the wooden stock was replaced by a folding metal version. The first of the metal stocks was a hinged two-section folding type that, when put away,

THE UZI EXPLODED

	Key		
1	Screw, stud cocking lever	**36**	Pistol grip, right half
2	Spring washer	**37**	Nut, foregrip
3	Stud, cocking lever handle	**38**	Foregrip, right half
4	Cocking handle	**39**	Foregrip, left half
5	Cover assembly	**40**	Screw, foregrip
6	Cocking lever	**41**	Spring, trigger frame
7	Spring, cocking lever	**42**	Sear
8	Breech-block	**43**	Pin, sear
9	Return spring assembly	**44**	Spring, trigger
10	Extractor	**45**	Trigger
11	Pin, extractor	**46**	Pin, trigger
12	Nut, screw backsight	**47**	Pin, intermediate sear lever
13	Backsight	**48**	Lever, intermediate, sear
14	Spring, backsight	**49**	Pin securing trigger frame
15	Body assembly	**50**	Catch, magazine
16	Screw, backsight	**51**	Spring, catch magazine
17	Barrel	**52**	Pin, catch magazine
18	Barrel retaining nut	**53**	Pistol grip, left half
19	Barrel catch	**54**	Screws, pistol grip
20	Spring control barrel catch	**55**	Magazine
21	Foresight	**56**	Magazine spring platform
22	Nut, foresight	**57**	Magazine spring
23	Spring washer, foresight	**58**	Magazine spring base
24	Catch, cover	**59**	Magazine baseplate
25	Spring, catch cover	**60**	Blade, bayonet
26	Catch, butt	**61**	Grip, right, bayonet
27	Screw, butt assembly catch	**62**	Screw assembly, bayonet
28	Metal butt assembly (folding)	**63**	Grip, left, bayonet
29	Quick-detachable wooden stock	**64**	Nut, screw assembly, bayonet
30	Housing for trigger group and magazine	**65**	Nut, plunger bayonet
31	Change lever	**66**	Spring, plunger bayonet
32	Spring, plunger safety	**67**	Plunger, bayonet
33	Automatic safety, pistol grip	**68**	Spring, scabbard bayonet
34	Spring, safety	**69**	Scabbard, bayonet
35	Knob, operating change lever	**70**	Screw, spring scabbard, bayonet

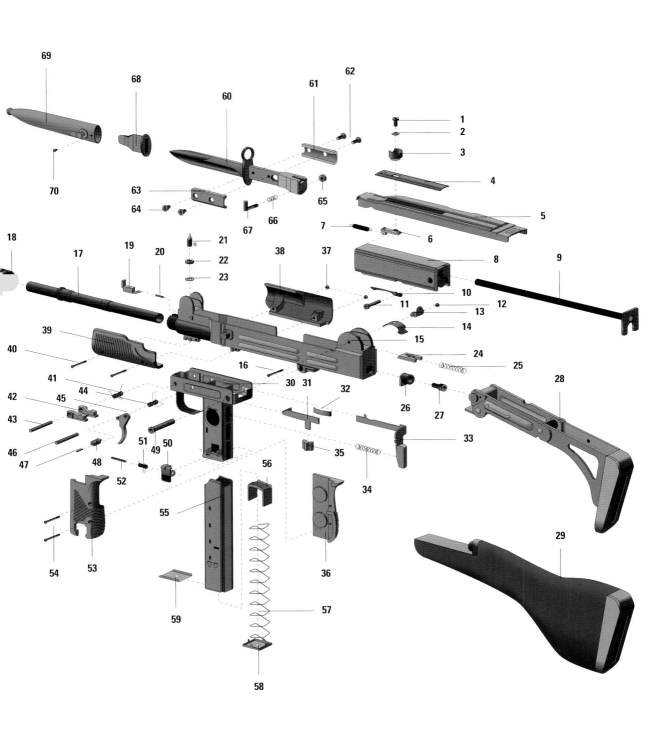

Security guards conduct a patrol with their Uzis. The shoulder straps are a useful addition, as they keep the Uzis perfectly ready at belt height, from where they could be fired from the hip if necessary. (Cody Images)

swung up flat beneath the rear of the receiver. To open this stock, the user simply slapped the butt plate in a downward and forward direction to disengage the stock from its holding catch; then he gripped the butt plate and pulled it rearwards, snapping out the stock until it locked into place. The system was durable and convenient (it also shaved 0.1kg off the gun's total weight), and it gave greater concealability and portability for special forces, paratroopers and security units. Over its lifetime, the Uzi has received several other types of stock, many within the context of civilian and security markets. These include modern polymer versions of the original wooden stocks, and plastic models with rubber butt plates.

Turning to sights, the original Uzi came with basic but functional factory-zeroed iron sights. The front sight consisted of a simple steel blade protected by two deep steel guards on either side. It was this sight that was adjustable for windage and elevation, requiring special tools to loosen the foresight screw and make the alterations. The rear sight, also protected by high metal wings, was a diopter type (a small, adjustable aperture), which could be flipped between 100m and 200m range as required. The sights were solid and dependable, worked effectively over the given ranges and gave rapid target acquisition for snap-shooting.

Uzis were available with two magazine types – a standard 25-round version with a fully loaded weight of 500g, and a larger capacity 32-round magazine weighing 600g. The length of the magazine was kept in check by a double-stack design.

In terms of general external appearance, the Uzi was a triumph of simplicity and combat-minded design. The magazine release catch sat on the bottom left side of the pistol grip, making it simple to reach with the thumb of the left hand, but kept out of the way during firing. Its receiver was a simple pressed-steel body, with fittings for an optional sling if required, and the cocking handle ran through a groove on the top of the receiver, within easy reach of the left hand. A short ribbed section beneath the front sight served as a foregrip, from which a short section of barrel protruded, held in place by a large barrel retaining nut. Accessories at first were limited, but they included a short bayonet, locked over the muzzle with a crossguard ring and engaged with a stud at the front of the foregrip.

EVOLUTION AND VARIANTS

The qualities of the Uzi, for both military and security use, soon caught the eye of international markets. Such was the confidence of IMI that in 1955 an Uzi was submitted into weapons trials against some of Europe's greatest submachine guns, the rival designs being the German MP 40, the Swedish Carl Gustav, the Danish Madsen and the British Sterling. All were decent 9mm designs, but only the Uzi survived the trial without being disqualified.

In 1956 came the Uzi's first big foreign order, when the Dutch Army bought thousands of Uzis as a complement to its standard infantry rifle, the 7.62×51mm NATO FN FAL. It quickly became clear to the authorities at IMI that the Uzi needed some additional manufacturing muscle behind it. Therefore, in 1958, IMI made an agreement with the Belgian manufacturer of the FN FAL, FN Herstal, who received a licence to produce and sell the Uzi, as long as all sales were approved by IMI in advance. The FN agreement helped galvanize the Uzi's distribution during the 1960s and 1970s, pitching military sales to special forces, paratroopers and vehicle crews – the latter benefited from the Uzi's small dimensions, which made it convenient to store within the confines of a tank or armoured personnel carrier.

Another boost for Uzi sales came in the 1960s with its adoption as the standard SMG for the US Secret Service. Furthermore, during the following decade Rhodesia also became one of the licensed producers of Uzis, giving the weapon greater access to African markets. A press statement by an IMI official in 1982 declared that since manufacture of the Uzi began in 1953 (in which year alone Israel made $600,000 worth of

The Uzi's export successes included Latin America. Here, a haul of weapons from Operation *Urgent Fury*, the US-led invasion of Grenada in 1983, includes this standard Uzi, with its barrel removed to render it useless to any potential resistance fighters. (Cody Images)

Uzis have seen all manner of service, conventional and unconventional. The Uzi Carbine here is held by a US Navy officer, who has acquired one for a weapons familiarization exercise on the carrier USS *Kitty Hawk* in 1983. (Cody Images)

small-arms exports), one million Uzis had been sold to foreign governments or law-enforcement agencies, contributing to IMI exports worth $300 million in 1981 alone. For large-scale orders, an individual Uzi was selling for about $350 on the export market in the early 1980s.

Despite the evident success of the Uzi, the 1970s and early 1980s began to bring a slowdown in sales globally (although as we shall see there were rises in specific markets). There were many factors involved, not least the explosive distribution of the AK-47 (about which we shall say more in the following chapter), and the mounting popularity of the American M16 assault rifle. The overthrow of the Shah of Iran in 1979 also wiped out another major customer. Domestic demand for the Uzi also went into a decline.

IMI's resolution of the problem was not only to foster new clients for the Uzi (which it did), but also to revive the Uzi design itself. In 1979, IMI introduced a civilian, semi-auto version of the Uzi, thereby neatly bypassing the ban on imports of military surplus weapons passed in the United States as part of the 1968 Gun Control Act. Distributed from 1980 in the United States by Action Arms, the semi-auto Uzi versions came with 409mm barrels to meet the minimum rifle barrel requirement for civilian weapons. (Action Arms also imported full-auto Uzis for the military and law-enforcement markets.) In addition, the weapons were fitted with the more complex closed-bolt system (see box opposite), which put up extra barriers to anyone furtively inclined to convert his weapon to full-auto. Two models of the 'Uzi Carbine' were shipped into the United States, Models A and B, the latter incorporating minor differences from the Model A in sight adjustment, firing pin safety mechanism, sling swivel stud and other features. In both civilian and security markets in the United States, the Uzi began to appear in different calibres to broaden its appeal, including .45 ACP, .22 LR (as a conversion kit) and .41 AE.

Mini and Micro Uzis

The greatest change in the direction of the Uzi came with the introduction of the Mini Uzi in 1980. To appeal more broadly to special forces and elite security units, IMI significantly reduced the dimensions of the standard weapon. The original Uzi has a stock-folded length of 470mm; the Mini Uzi takes that down to just 360mm. Weight is reduced by replacing the relatively heavy two-section folding stock of the standard Uzi with a lightweight one-piece wire stock, fitted to the receiver via a hinged bracket.

Compared to the standard Uzi, the Mini Uzi also has critical differences in its internal workings. Most significantly, the gun is available in either open-bolt or closed-bolt configurations. In the open-bolt version, the firing pin remains an integral part of the breech-block, as on the conventional Uzi. In the closed-bolt weapon, the breech-block features a separate spring-loaded firing pin, carried by a firing-pin guide. Cocking the weapon chambers a round, with the bolt seated around the breech, and pulling the trigger releases just the firing pin, resulting in a faster lock time (the time between pulling the trigger and a cartridge firing) and therefore a more accurate and stable shooting platform.

There are several external differences between the Mini and standard Uzi, apart from the reduction in dimensions. The sights are redesigned, with both the front and rear sights being adjustable. At the barrel end, a noticeable distinction is a muzzle compensator, consisting of two

Open bolt and closed bolt

Whether a gun fires from an open bolt or a closed bolt is a central decision in the design of a submachine gun. An open bolt is held back from the breech prior to firing, so when the trigger is pulled the bolt runs forward (under the pressure of the return spring), strips a cartridge from the magazine, chambers and fires it, all in one movement. The advantage of the open bolt is that there are fewer moving parts involved, making the gun simpler to manufacture and maintain. Open-bolt guns also stay cooler under intense firing, reducing the risk of a round in the chamber 'cooking-off' from barrel heat, and the user doesn't have to pull a bolt back against a stiff return spring to clear the chamber if necessary. The key disadvantage with an open-bolt gun is that there is a heavy shift of mass when the trigger is pulled, as the bolt slams forward, and combined with generally increased vibrations

such guns tend to be inaccurate, and hard to keep on target. Closed-bolt guns chamber the first round when the gun is cocked, with the bolt forward and seated on the breech. When the trigger is pulled, only the firing pin (or hammer) and its spring move forward, both of light mass and therefore having minimal effect on the point of aim. Closed-bolt guns are known for their accuracy, particularly important in very fast-firing SMGs. Closed-bolt guns are generally more complex than open-bolt guns, so they tend to cost more to produce and are more demanding to maintain, with increased possibilities of jamming. Such guns are also in greater danger of overheating and cooking-off rounds, although this issue is rarely a problem in SMGs, as the atmospheric pressure of pistol cartridges is generally insufficient to cause adverse temperature build-up.

ABOVE This dismantled closed-bolt Mini Uzi provides a good view of the main parts, including the long recoil spring pointing directly into the firing-pin guide. The butt of the folding stock projects down from the right side of the receiver. (Israel Weapon Industries)

The Mini Uzi seen in full profile, with its side-swinging folding stock extended. The selector switch is in the 'S' safe position, and the gun has Picatinny rails mounted on the top and beneath the muzzle. (Israel Weapon Industries)

This close-up view of a Micro Uzi shows just how compact the weapon is. Despite its size, it is still capable of controlled fire at cyclical rates of up to 1,700rpm. (Cody Images)

compensating vent slots cut into the top of the barrel, which divert gas upward to counteract barrel climb during full-auto fire. Such a feature was necessary on the Mini Uzi, as the reduction in weight of its internal moving parts, plus design refinements, give it an official cyclical rate of fire of around 1,100rpm – this means that it can run through a 32-round magazine in just over two seconds. Note also that although the Mini Uzi could take the standard 25- and 32-round Uzi magazines, a special 20-round magazine was also made available.

Such impressive firepower was clearly aimed at the law-enforcement and security services, and the US market for the guns was again tapped into via the Uzi importer Action Arms. By the mid-1980s, the US Mini Uzis were available in closed-bolt, open-bolt and heavy-bolt versions, the latter reducing the gun's rate of fire. Action Arms also began importing a semi-auto version in 1987, to bypass federal firearms regulations and sell the Mini Uzi to the civilian market.

Yet the Uzi's reduction in size was by no means finished. In 1986 IMI unveiled an even smaller version – the appropriately named Micro Uzi. In this version, the dimensions strained down towards the limits of ingenuity. With its stock extended, the original Micro Uzi measured 486mm, but with the stock folded forward against the receiver the total length from the muzzle to the end of the receiver was just 282mm. Empty weight was a mere 2.2kg (the original Uzi had weighed 3.6kg). The original Micro Uzi, firing from an open bolt, had an impressive rate of fire of up to 1,700rpm, although in later closed-bolt models this was reduced to 1,050rpm.

Mini and Micro Uzi data

Mechanical features	Mini Uzi OB (STD)	Mini Uzi CB (STD)	Mini Uzi CB (SF)	Micro Uzi CB (SF)
Cartridge	9×19mm Parabellum			
Operation	Blowback, selective fire OBP or CBP*			
Firing mode	Semi-auto, auto			
Feeding	20-, 25- and 32-round box magazine			
Barrel rifling	4 grooves, right-hand twist, 1 turn in 254mm			
Weight				
Weapon only	2.65kg	2.65kg	2.80kg	2.20kg
Lengths				
Barrel	197mm	197mm	197mm	134mm
Overall length – stock extended	588mm	588mm	588mm	504mm
Overall length – stock folded	360mm	360mm	360mm	282mm
Firing characteristics				
Muzzle velocity (approx.)	380m/sec	380m/sec	380m/sec	350m/sec
Rate of fire (approx.)	1,100rpm	1,150rpm	1,150rpm	1,050rpm
Sight				
Sight line radius	235 degrees	235 degrees	235 degrees	184 degrees
Front sight	Post type (adjustable for elevation)			
Rear sight	Aperture, 'L' flip type (adjustable for windage)			
Silencer option	Yes	No	No	Yes

* OBP = Open-bolt position; CBP = Closed-bolt position

Source: IWI document 'Mini and Micro Uzi SMG 9mm'.

The new Micro Uzi offered a uniquely powerful but controllable SMG to the special forces and law-enforcement worlds, and alongside the Mini Uzi it remains a popular product to this day. In fact, only the Mini and Micro Uzi remain in production with Israel Weapon Industries (IWI), although standard Uzis are still available as refurbished models. (IWI was originally part of IMI, but it was bought by the SK Group in 2005, since when it has been operating as a private company.) Full-size Uzis are also manufactured under licence in the United States.

Both the Mini and Micro Uzis offered platforms for additional improvements, including 'Special Forces' (SF) versions with Picatinny rails (an extremely popular and flexible rail system for mounting accessories) fitted. In recent years, IWI also brought out a new version of the Micro Uzi, specially created for use by Israeli elite units, particularly those involved with hostage-rescue operations and other close-quarters battle (CQB) actions. Known as the Uzi Pro, it operates on the same principles as the closed-bolt Micro Uzi, but with some distinct enhancements in terms of furniture and layout. One of the most obvious changes is the 'assault grip', essentially a large extended trigger guard in thick, impact-resistant black polymer. This extends down to the bottom of the pistol grip, allowing the gun to be used comfortably with all manner of gloves. (Among the principal

The Uzi Pro is a major new incarnation of the Uzi, revealed for the first time at the Eurosatory show in 2010. Its integral Picatinny rails make it capable of multiple different configurations. (Israel Weapon Industries)

clients for the Uzi Pro are Israel's fast-roping hostage-rescue teams, who by the nature of their deployment technique must wear gloves to protect their hands from rope abrasion.) The hand guard extends up under the front of the receiver and barrel, where it forms a mount for taking flashlights and laser pointers. In total, the Uzi Pro has no fewer than four Picatinny rails mounted around its small frame to take a variety of optical and night-vision sights, and other combat tools to enhance its performance. The largest of the rails is mounted on the top of the gun, so the cocking handle has been moved from the top of the receiver to the left-hand side. (The Mini Uzi is also now available with side-cocking.)

The Uzi Pro has a host of other features to enhance its CQB performance, and maintain its relevance to special forces. Its barrel is threaded to take a suppressor if required. In fact, a variety of suppressors have been and are available for all sizes of Uzi, although their fitment can radically alter the centre of balance on such a small weapon. The standard front and rear sights are self-illuminating for night-time use.

The Uzi Pistol

Another Uzi variant deserving of a special mention, this time looking back to the commercial civilian market, is the Uzi Pistol. Here was another scaled-down Uzi, produced by IMI during the early 1980s and brought to the US market by Action Arms in 1984. As its title suggests, this weapon is a de facto semi-auto pistol, although it is still very recognizably of the Uzi stable. In its shortening, the Uzi Pistol exceeds even the compression of the Micro Uzi, measuring a mere 240mm from the rear of the receiver to the muzzle – it is not fitted with a folding stock.

The Uzi Pistol, essentially a semi-auto-only Micro Uzi without a stock. (Terry Ashe/Time & Life Pictures/Getty Images)

As an aside, it is interesting to look at the reductions in barrel length between the standard Uzi and the Uzi Pistol. While the standard Uzi has a 260mm barrel, the Mini Uzi reduced this to 197mm and the Micro Uzi still further to 134mm. At only 115mm, the barrel of the Uzi Pistol is less than half the length of the original Uzi's, and in fact is only 1mm longer than that of a Glock 17 pistol. The weapon illustrates how easily Uziel Gal's early design could be scaled down, depending on requirements.

This whistle-stop tour through the principal versions of the Uzi SMG does not entirely do justice to the variations on a theme that have characterized the Uzi range. By having a life in both civilian and military markets, and in its negotiations of various firearms laws in the United States and other places, the Uzi has seen all manner of local modifications and prototypes – even a version capable of firing rifle grenades. The huge range of accessories available can also transform the Uzi in both appearance and performance, not always positively in the most excessive examples. The Uzi has further been offered, as we have seen, in a variety of calibres, and non-standard conversion kits can widen the range of available calibres to include .40 S&W and 10mm Auto.

What cannot be doubted, however, is the weapon's overall success in the marketplace. During its heyday beween the 1960s and the 1980s, it became the world's most popular SMG for law enforcement and special forces, only gradually bumped from the top slot by the Heckler & Koch MP5. Including all variants and unlicensed copies, more than ten million units have been made, making it one of history's most mass-produced weapons.

USE
Desert warfare to gang warfare

Recently, I was walking my dog down the local farm track, when I bumped into a friend, former Rhodesian African Rifles soldier Alan James. Having interviewed Alan before about his experience of fighting in the Rhodesian bush war of the 1970s and early 1980s, and knowing about the licensed manufacture of Uzis in Rhodesia, I asked him about his experience of the weapon. He confessed that he had never carried one on official military operations, but he did own one, like many Rhodesian farmers, as a private security weapon. It had been fired in anger – on one occasion Alan let fly with a long rippling burst that slashed through the grasses on his farm, serving as a lethal warning to insurgents around his property. Having shared this simple story, we parted ways, only for Alan to turn and shout back to me over a good distance: 'I've never known the Uzi to jam.' For an ex-soldier, such a simple point was critical – the gun that jams easily can cost you your life in combat. Here was just one of the reasons why the Uzi went on to have a distribution numbered not just in thousands of weapons, but millions.

Regardless of the period of post-war history, or the variant of weapon involved, the Uzi has always built its reputation on four factors: portability, reliability, ease of use, and firepower. All four of these attributes would be proven in the conflicts in which Israel was immersed from the early 1950s to the 1970s. As we shall see, the Uzi has survived the ultimate battlefield tests, in environments that would choke many guns to a halt.

FIRING THE UZI
Before exploring the operational history of the Uzi in greater detail, we need to be clear about how it is used. The explanation below applies to

almost any model of Uzi, with some obvious differences in terms of the positioning of cocking handles or whether a gun fires full-auto or semi-auto only. By describing the firing procedure, we begin to define how and why the Uzi has been such a long-standing favourite of people who put their lives on the line.

Firing the Uzi of course first demands that the user has a full magazine. Typically, these are hand-loaded, the operator holding the magazine in one hand while pushing 9mm cartridges one by one down past the magazine lips with the other, onto the magazine platform spring. Autoloaders have also been available in modern times, these consisting of mechanical devices that fit on top of the magazine, and use a lever action to feed rounds down into the magazine at a much faster rate. The modern Lula autoloader (designed for the Israeli military), for example, can fill a 30-round Uzi magazine in 35 seconds, and its action can be reversed for unloading – the same 30-round magazine can be emptied in five seconds using the device.

Once the magazine is charged, it is simply slipped into the housing within the Uzi's pistol grip, and pushed up until it engages positively with the magazine catch. As mentioned above, the Uzi follows a straightforward hand-meets-hand procedure of magazine insertion, making it an instinctive action with only limited practice, and one that can be performed extremely quickly under stress. Usually, the gun is canted about 60 degrees to the right to expose the magazine housing more openly to the user.

Cocking the weapon is, for a right-handed person (the Uzi is best suited to right-handed operation), a matter of gripping the cocking handle, drawing it to the rear of its travel, then releasing. While, on the open-bolt guns, the breech-block remains at the rear, the cocking lever nevertheless returns to its forward position via a spring. Assuming that the fire selector is at 'S', all that remains to fire the gun is to push the selector to either 'A' or 'R', depending on the desired mode of fire. (Simply holding the gun disengages the integral safety on the back of the grip.)

Here we see the correct magazine loading procedure for an Uzi-type weapon, with the gun held in the right hand and canted to about 60 degrees, while the magazine is inserted into the aperture at the base of the pistol grip. (Israel Weapon Industries)

27

The cocking action on the Mini Uzi is the same as with all Uzi weapons. Here the cocking lever on the top of the weapon is drawn back; the opening breech-block can be seen through the ejection port on the side of the receiver. (Israel Weapon Industries)

Despite its high rate of fire, the Uzi fires controllably if it is handled correctly, with the shooter leaning his weight into the gun and letting off manageable bursts, typically about 5–10 rounds intermittently. Longer bursts will generally result in muzzle climb or excessive wobble, but professional soldiers and security personnel rarely want to burn through their magazine too quickly. The orthodox firing position is with the Uzi shouldered, stock extended, as this position allows full use of the sights. With the iron sights, the front post is aligned with the target through the centre of the rear aperture. Such is the weapon's balance, however, that it can be fired easily from the hip in trained hands, the user aiming by natural sense of direction plus adjustment of the observed impact of the bullets. In low-light or smoky conditions, modern fittings such as flashlights and laser pointers are further guides to aim.

One-handed firing, while perfectly possibly for someone who is extremely familiar with handling the gun, is typically not recommended if only for reasons of accuracy – such fire would be largely a matter of 'spray and pray'. A distinct advantage of the Uzi, however, is that it can be carried one-handed prior to firing (which is much more difficult to do with a full-length assault rifle or two-handed submachine gun). This facility is more important than it at first appears. Running, for example, is slowed by holding a weapon in both hands, as it keeps both arms to the front and prevents their swinging momentum that adds extra speed to the run.

Five or six controlled bursts will usually empty an Uzi 32-round magazine, the spent cartridges ejecting from the port on the right of the gun, and following an up-and-to-the-right trajectory. On open-bolt guns, when the magazine runs out and the trigger is pulled 'dry' the bolt stops in the front position and the magazine needs changing. This is largely a repeat of the loading procedure, once the spent magazine has been ejected by pressing the release catch on the grip. On occasions the bolt will actually stop in the rear position, such as when release of the trigger in automatic fire coincides with firing the last round in the magazine. In such occasions, the gun does not need to be cocked again to fire, once a fresh magazine is inserted.

MAINTENANCE

As the earlier statement from Alan James indicates, the Uzi is an exceptionally reliable gun, with tolerances loose enough to cope with the ingress of sand and all manner of debris. We should not push the point too far – the Uzi, like all firearms, can and will jam if not given a diligent programme of cleaning and maintenance. An early IMI manual gave the following instructions for handling an Uzi malfunction:

> Remove magazine and wait 3 seconds with barrel pointing in a safe direction, then inspect magazine.[2]
>
> 1. MAGAZINE EMPTY
> Cock to remove possible last round. Inspect the chamber and if empty, insert full magazine, recock and continue firing.
>
> 2. MAGAZINE NOT EMPTY
> (Malfunction)
> a. Recock to clear possible defective or wrongly positioned round. If a round or case ejects, inspect chamber and if empty, reload and continue firing.
> b. If nothing ejects, fully draw back bolt and check if a cartridge or case is in the chamber. If empty, reload and continue firing.
> c. If base of cartridge is visible, fire in a safe direction. If weapon fires and ejects, reload and continue.
> d. If weapon does not fire, set fire selector 'S' (Safe) and follow trouble shooting procedure for 'spent case of round stuck in chamber'.[3]

For the latter situation, the manual goes on to explain, more drastic action is required. It involves removing the bolt assembly, then pushing a cleaning rod through the barrel from the front to remove any obstruction in the chamber or bore. Once both are clear, they are then cleaned and reassembled; if the gun still stubbornly refuses to fire, then a visit to the armourer is required. The immediate action clearance procedure would be second nature to a well-trained soldier or law-enforcement officer, and could be performed in a matter of seconds. If the problem was more serious, and it rarely was, in a combat situation the soldier would generally switch to a backup weapon such as a handgun, rather than resort to advanced maintenance. (Note that one of the principal causes of Uzis jamming is defective ammunition, always a risk in a gun that uses one of the most common types of cartridge in the world, manufactured in a variety of places and under different factory conditions.)

---

[2] The reason for waiting three seconds and controlling the barrel direction is in case a cartridge primer has partially ignited, the primer smouldering until it finally triggers main charge detonation

[3] Israel Military Industries Ltd, *Uzi 9mm Submachine Gun: Instruction Manual*, Ramat Hasharon: IWI (n.d.) p.34

Here the operator is lifting clear the breech-block of a closed-bolt Uzi. Note the deep cut in the side of the breech-block, through which spent cartridge cases are ejected. Also note the muzzle compensator grooves at the front of the gun, designed to control muzzle climb during full-auto fire. (Israel Weapon Industries)

In terms of regular maintenance, a professional soldier would field strip his Uzi after each session of use, clean any powder deposits from the barrel, chamber and breech-block and lightly oil any moving parts. Oiling, as soldiers from the Middle East know better than most, should not be overdone, as the oil will attract sand and dust and turn itself into an abrasive grinding paste, wearing away at delicate parts. Field stripping the Uzi, while tedious to describe in detail, is a simple and intuitive process. The receiver cover (the top part of the receiver, holding the cocking handle), for example, is removed simply by pressing the cover catch at the rear of the gun and lifting the cover up and out. This exposes the breech-block, which can now be taken clear out of the gun. Removing the barrel is also straightforward: a barrel catch near the front sight is first pushed to the rear, then the barrel nut can be unscrewed.

To open the Uzi's receiver for field stripping, first the top cover catch is pulled to the rear. Here the top cover is fitted with a Picatinny rail, hence the cocking lever is on the left side of the gun, not the top. (Israel Weapon Industries)

Once the Uzi's top cover has been released, it can be lifted up and clear of the weapon, exposing the breech-block beneath – here in its forward position under the tension of the return spring. (Israel Weapon Industries)

In fact, the procedures just described constitute much of the basic field stripping procedure a soldier needed to know – more extensive maintenance to parts such as the extractor and trigger mechanisms required a higher degree of knowledge, although one many soldiers and professionals would possess.

THE UZI IN ACTION 1956–67

Following the War of Independence in 1948, the IDF moved into a period of restructuring and consolidation, as it sought to build itself into a modern, professional army capable of dealing with the threats that remained just across its borders. Units and formations were given formal organization, and processes of logistics and training were rationalized. A system of reservist mobilization was put in place, which involved reserve officers and NCOs being called to action via telephone and telegram, after which they activated the other ranks literally by word of mouth. By 1956, this procedure was capable of bringing 100,000 reservists into action in less than a day. Importantly, the IDF undertook the rationalization of equipment and weaponry described above, which included introducing the Uzi.

It must be acknowledged that although the Uzi became a standard-issue IDF submachine gun from 1955, it was never the general personal weapon of most Israeli soldiers. That honour fell to the Belgian 7.62×51mm FN FAL rifle (although it took time for complete issue to take place). The FAL couldn't have been much more different from the Uzi. It measured 1,053mm in length, and weighed 4.31kg empty. It had a 20-round magazine and fired its rounds at a muzzle velocity nearly three times greater than that produced by the Uzi. While the Uzi's practical range would become strained beyond 200m, the FAL was perfectly capable of reaching out to beyond 600m, and taking someone down with considerable force.

The FAL was a fine weapon, of that there was no doubt, but it was not ideal for all users. It was heavy and unsuited to close-quarters combat (rather like the bolt-action rifles of old), and not easy to store inside an armoured vehicle or in the cab of a truck. For such reasons, the first Uzis issued to the IDF gravitated towards airborne soldiers, special forces and vehicle crews, although as production increased they went increasingly into the Israeli Army at large, to bolster squad CQB firepower.

The first major war in which the Uzi would serve occurred in 1956, but it was proving its utility before that date. Despite its victory in the War of Independence, Israel was ringed with avowed enemies – Egypt, Syria and Jordan – who promised to extinguish the nascent state. During the late 1940s, these enemies began to make increasingly confident cross-border raids, which in turn inspired Israeli retaliations. Initial Israeli responses were heavy-handed and ineffective, leading the IDF high command to form unorthodox groups of commandos such as, in 1953, Unit 101, led by the powerful figure of Ariel Sharon. Early photographs of this unit show its soldiers using a mix of ageing submachine guns, such as Stens and MP 40s.

In 1954 Moshe Dayan, the IDF Chief of Staff, merged Unit 101 with the 890th Battalion (the IDF's first airborne unit) to create a brigade-strength Unit 202 (renamed the Paratroop Brigade in 1957), which Dayan hoped would combine Unit 101's daring with the paras' discipline. He was not to be disappointed. The paratroopers pioneered new infiltration and attack tactics, to be used against Arab outposts, barracks and other military buildings. Moreover, the paras took the Uzi as a standard weapon. The short-range firepower of the Uzi was ideal for night-time operations – covert actions were rarely launched in the day – as under conditions of darkness the ranges of combat shorten significantly. The tactical goal of most missions was to approach to the closest possible range before opening up with overwhelming bursts of Uzi crossfire, and working through buildings, bunkers and trenches.

The Uzi excelled in this role, being easy to carry and aim, beating rifle-armed Arab soldiers to the shot at close ranges. Other elements of the unit would also stake out approach routes to the main action, from where they would ambush poorly deployed Arab reinforcements. The excellence of the new tactics, and of the Uzi, was demonstrated in Operation *Shomron*, an Uzi-armed airborne forces raid on the Kilkilya Police Station in Jordan. During the attack, a police fort and its garrison were destroyed on the night of 10 October 1956, although the Israeli troops themselves suffered 18 killed.

The early battles with the Uzi in the 1950s proved its worth in both concept and practice. In 1956, a far larger conflict would test out the Uzi on a broader scale. On 29 October 1956, Israeli forces moved into the Sinai Desert in force, fighting against four Egyptian infantry divisions in their way. The invasion was part of a secret, and complicated, agreement with France and Britain, who themselves intervened militarily in the region to undo Gamal Abdel Nasser's nationalization of the Suez Canal.

Although the 'Suez Crisis' would prove to be an ignominious failure for France and Britain, for Israel it was a primary opportunity to demonstrate what it could now achieve in conventional warfare. A key part of the plan was for Israeli paratroopers to make an advance air drop into the Sinai Desert and secure the strategically important Mitla Pass, holding it for advancing IDF armoured forces. Known as Operation *Kadesh*, the action to clear the Mitla Pass deteriorated into an exhausting and bloody close-quarters slog, Israeli troops of the Na'ha'l 88th Battalion (part of Unit 202) having to clear the Egyptian soldiers from numerous caves dotted around the pass. It was found that the best way of doing this was a barrage of hand grenades lobbed through the cave entrance, followed by scything blasts of Uzi fire. Only on 31 October did the Mitla Pass finally fall into Israeli hands; 260 Egyptians were dead, while Unit 202 suffered 38 dead and 120 wounded.

An Israeli unit conducts vehicular reconnaissance near the Gaza border in 1955. The Uzi held by the man on the right would have been one of the first models issued to the IDF. (Cody Images)

More than anything, it was the action at the Mitla Pass that put the Uzi on the map with the IDF, and the wider world. Its demonstration of close-range firepower, and its trustworthiness under the most adverse of conditions, gave those to whom it was issued well-founded confidence.

The Six-Day War

Between 1956 and the next major regional conflict, the Six-Day War of 1967, the Uzi continued to excel in the context of the ongoing bubbling conflict between Israel and its Arab neighbours, and the rise of Palestinian armed activism under Yasser Arafat's Fatah movement. Elite *Sayeret*

This photo, taken during the Six-Day War of 1967, shows the classic blend of infantry firepower in the IDF at this time. The two soldiers to the right carry FN FAL rifles, while those behind can provide close-range full-auto firepower from their Uzis. (Getty Images)

special forces units took their Uzis out on numerous raiding and counter-terrorism operations, with solid results. Yet the Six-Day War was to have the most profound effect on the Uzi, and its place within the Israeli military. Prior to the conflict, the Uzi was a standard-issue weapon, used heavily throughout the IDF. Following the war, the IDF would begin to distance itself from the Uzi in preference for an entirely different type of weapon, although the Uzi would remain in thriving use with Israeli special forces units for years to come.

The Six-Day War of 1967, as history now knows, was a campaign of military brilliance by the IDF. In a pre-emptive combined-arms operation, the Israeli forces roundly defeated the armies of Egypt, Jordan and Syria and took control of the Gaza Strip, the Sinai Peninsula, the West Bank, East Jerusalem and the Golan Heights.

During this conflict, the Uzi was involved in thousands of engagements, from clashes in the open expanses of the Sinai Desert through to street fighting in the alleyways of Jerusalem. As in the 1956 war, the Uzi affirmed its reliability and firepower under extreme combat conditions. Eric Hammel, in his history of the Six-Day War, here describes an assault by Israeli paratroopers on an Egyptian position:

> Under cover of the preliminary Israeli artillery barrage, the four groups of Israeli paratroopers had infiltrated into the northern edge of the Egyptian artillery sector, a task that was made much easier by the lack of an all-around protected trenchline. As the battle for the trenchlines began, one group of Israeli paratroopers was detected, but, firing their Uzi submachine guns from the hip, the remainder rushed 200 meters into the nearest gun pits and shot or chased away all the crewmen.[4]

[4] Eric Hammel, *Six Days in June: How Israel won the 1967 Arab-Israeli War*, New York: Scribner's (1992) p.238

A common theme in many accounts of Uzi use during the Six-Day War – and other conflicts – is that firing from the hip while on the move was common. The FN FAL rifle is difficult to wield in the same manner, not only on account of its length but also because of its hefty recoil. With the rear of the receiver pressed against the side of the stomach, the Uzi was stable even when fired at a sprint pace, which enabled fast snap-shooting and allowed Israeli soldiers to deliver their own fire support as they closed on enemy positions.

For all these reasons, the Uzi really came into its own in the struggles for the rocky Golan Heights in Syria. The Syrians not only had the support of the Golan Heights' tortuous terrain, with precipitous slopes, rocky surfaces and numerous interlacing streams, but they had also built an extensive system of fortified defences into the rock. One advantage the IDF had, however, was the Uzi. During the frenzy of bunker assaults and attacks through Syrian trenches, the Uzi's compact configuration and firepower were ideal. On many occasions, Israeli soldiers would beat Syrian troops, armed primarily with heavier AK-47s, to the shot, and though many other factors were involved, the Uzi undoubtedly contributed to a hard-fought Israeli victory in that sector.

A wounded IDF soldier, his Uzi slung by his side on a shoulder strap, is helped by a comrade near the Suez Canal in 1967. (Cody Images)

In urban combat during the Six-Day War, the Uzi was equally decisive for largely the same reasons as described above. The following account comes from the battle for Jerusalem, in which an Israeli paratrooper describes the moment when he encountered a Jordanian soldier, and knew he had to act quickly:

> We looked at each other for half a second and I knew that it was up to me, personally, to kill him, there was no one else there. The whole thing must have lasted less than a second, but it's printed on my mind like a slow-motion movie. I fired from the hip and I can still see the bullets splashed against the wall about a meter to his left. I moved the Uzi slowly, slowly it seemed, until I hit him in the body. He slipped to his knees, then he raised his head, with his face terrible, twisted in pain and hate, yes such hate. I fired again and somehow got him in the head. There was so much blood … I vomited until the rest of the boys came up.[5]

[5] Quoted in Jeremy Bowen, *Six Days: How the 1967 War Shaped the Middle East*, London: Simon & Schuster (2003) p.180

IDF soldiers rest during operations around the Suez Canal in the late 1960s. The Uzi-armed soldier on the right has numerous additional magazines in the pouches at the front of his web belt. (Cody Images)

This powerful account cautions us against discussing the Uzi in too mechanical a fashion. It reminds us that such weapons are ultimately killing machines, and that using one in earnest has a profound psychological effect on the user, as well as a gruesome physiological effect on the victim. The effect on the target is, indeed, part of the Uzi's *raison d'être*. Modern terminal ballistics studies have demonstrated that the idea that someone hit by one or two bullets simply drops on the spot and dies is a myth largely put about by Hollywood films. As many soldiers and police officers will recount, opponents have often been shot several times – and even sustained wounds that later prove mortal – but still keep functioning and fighting for many more seconds, even minutes, sometimes entirely unaware that they have been shot. Unless a direct hit occurs on the brain or central nervous system, the only way to bring someone down quickly is to accelerate the volume of blood loss through multiple hits to the central torso. (It is for this reason that modern law-enforcement training, at least in places such as the United States, tends now to emphasize a policy of repeatedly shooting an assailant until he or she is down on the ground, rather than following the 'double-tap' policy adopted in the 1970s and '80s.)

IDF paratroopers, Jerusalem, 1967 (previous pages)

A team of Israeli paratroopers fight a street battle in East Jerusalem during the 1967 Six-Day War. They are all armed with Uzis, some with the wooden stock version, but most with the newer folding stock type, and all have magazine pouches on their belts. The soldier on the far right has this stock in a collapsed position – a strike on the butt plate would free it from its locking catch, then it could be extended out to snap into place. Opposite, the soldier on the far left is reloading his Uzi, canting the gun to the right and slipping a fresh magazine in place. At the front, a soldier is engaging a target in an upper window, using sighted fire. First-hand accounts also state that the Uzi was frequently fired from the hip, the soldier adjusting the point of aim by 'walking' the observed impacts onto the target. The Uzi's ability to be fired in both ways made it ideally suited to urban combat, and often gave Israeli forces a firepower advantage in the narrow streets of Jerusalem. The gun's safety features were also an asset, as they reduced the chances of an accidental discharge in such close proximity to one's comrades.

The Uzi's rate of fire can seem excessive to civilians, but not so to many soldiers who have used it. A half-second burst delivers around seven rounds, which if on target will by itself be enough to bring down even the most determined individual. This is why the Uzi became a favoured weapon of special forces the world over – in a hostage-rescue situation, when a terrorist could kill dozens of hostages in his few last seconds of breath, a firearm with decisive takedown power is essential.

Another element to emerge out of the account is the way the Uzi is used, repeating the earlier emphasis on the gun being fired from the hip, and the way observed bullet strikes are used to 'walk' rounds onto the target. Although this is certainly not the most accurate way to use the Uzi, it does appear to be instinctive, the short dimensions of the gun and its low-recoil characteristics making out-of-shoulder shooting convenient and comfortable.

REPLACING THE UZI

As we have seen, the Uzi proved to be the best weapon for the job in many actions during the Six-Day War. Ironically, the conflict provided a quite different general message to the leadership of the IDF. The Six-Day War was the first time that the Israelis had come up against the Soviet AK-47 in any significant numbers. From the mid-1950s and through the 1960s, Soviet arms supplies to the Arab world surged to profound levels. Egypt received more than $500 million of Soviet weaponry between 1955 and 1960 alone, and $700 million worth in 1961–64. Syria also took millions of dollars' worth of Soviet military exports. These massive shipments included large volumes of AKM assault rifles (the modernized version of the classic AK-47), which IDF troops confronted first-hand during the Six-Day War.

Israeli troops pose outside the UN Headquarters in Jerusalem, during the Six-Day War. They carry a mix of old and new weapons, including folding-stock Uzis alongside FN FAL rifles and more venerable firearms. (Getty Images)

Even though the war in 1967 was a great Israeli victory, soldiers' confrontations with the AK were sobering. Firing a 7.62×39mm intermediate round, it offered the controllable recoil that made full-auto firepower viable, something that couldn't always be said of the FN FAL rifle with its powerful long-range rifle cartridge. The lighter cartridges also meant that an infantryman could carry more ammunition into battle. Yet the AK also outranged the Uzi significantly, being able to put down effective fire at distances of 350m and beyond. Added to this situation were the AK's legendary reliability and simplicity – IDF troops experienced not infrequent failures in the FAL in the dusty conditions of the Six-Day War, but noted that enemy AKs rarely misfired. Factor in the AK's snowballing mass production, which would make it the world's most prolific firearm, and it became clear to the IDF that a new Israeli standard-issue weapon was needed, one that fulfilled the roles of both the FAL and the Uzi.

At this particular time in history, the SMG was beginning to feel its age as a concept. The emerging generation of assault rifles, such as the AK and the American 5.56mm M16, offered heavy firepower over realistic combat ranges, in a relatively light package. For these reasons, during the early 1970s the IDF opened up a competition to find a new assault rifle for the Israeli armed services.

Five weapons were entered into the competition, either as assessment weapons or competitors – the AK, M16A1, Stoner 62, Heckler & Koch HK33, a new design by Yisrael Galili (who had previously made some contributions to the design of the Uzi) and an improved version of the Uzi by none other than Uziel Gal, who naturally saw a threat to his design. All weapons were tested in the most severe conditions possible, and their performance was assessed critically against the best international benchmarks. The nature of these tests is clear from the later accounts of Galili himself:

An Israeli patrol is conducted from a vehicle in Kuneitra City, Syria. The compact Uzi could be stowed conveniently in the cab of a truck or jeep, or inside an APC or tank, even without its folding stock configuration. (Cody Images)

As a standard IDF weapon the Uzi (along with the FN FAL) was replaced by the 5.56mm Galil, several of which are seen here being hung on the back door of a 155mm self-propelled gun stationed on the Israeli–Lebanese border in 2003. (Getty Images)

We had to build special machines and tools in order to test the rifle. We built a special machine to whirl and blow sand and dust on the gun. Also a special machine to make small caliber barrels, something we were trying to produce for the first time. The quantities of 5.56 caliber ammunition were dull [*sic*] and we had to purchase new ammunition to fill our magazine stocks. In spite of all the hardships, in a short time, we successfully finished a prototype and presented it to the IDF developing committee. In a firing range demonstration done by the committee, the Galil fired hundreds of rounds without a single stoppage.

Afterwards we delivered five rifles for testing with 30 and 50 rounds magazines. In the technical trials some problems occurred and had to be fixed and some features needed improvement. Thereafter, a new series of development sessions began on the rifle with the intent to improve its performances. A second comparative test was performed to test the Galil against the AK-47, M-16 and Stoner-63. There were drop tests, sand test, mud test, and many more. After all of these tests were completed, finally an endurance test of 18000 rounds was carried out. After passing all the technical tests, the next step was operational tests. The strict operational testing produced some suggestions for improvements and these changes were incorporated into the rifle.[6]

In 1973, after prolonged trials, the winner was revealed – the Galil rifle. At its heart, the Galil was indebted to the AK's rotating-bolt, gas-operated design (it was also influenced by the Finnish Valmet M62), but the weapon was calibrated for the 5.56×45mm NATO round. This cartridge was the same as that used by the US M16, which made ammunition deals between Israel and the United States much easier. It came with a folding stock, to make for more convenient storage in vehicles, and it had a 650rpm rate of fire. Accurate range was 500m-plus. As a practical battlefield weapon for the general soldiery, the Galil outclassed the Uzi on most levels.

[6] IWI, 2005

The Brazilian armed forces are among the Latin American military users of the Uzi. Here, a visit, board, search and seizure team of the frigate *Independencia* rappel onto their ship during a training exercise. (US Navy)

The rejection of the Uzi for the Galil appears to have affected Uziel Gal deeply (Gal had by this time risen to the rank of lieutenant-colonel). Just three years later he resigned from the IDF, and emigrated to the United States, where he lived in Philadelphia. Nevertheless, Israel was and remained enormously appreciative of the contribution that Gal had made to the defence of his country; in 1958 he had been awarded the prestigious Israel Security Award. In the United States, this humble man lived a quiet life working on various personal firearms projects, and he died on 7 September 2002.

IN SPECIAL FORCES SERVICE

Although the Uzi was no longer a standard-issue weapon, that fact in no way meant that it had been removed from Israeli service altogether.[7] During the 1973 Yom Kippur War it was still very much in action, either as stock that had not been replaced or, more often, as the weapon preferred by vehicle crews, particularly those hunkered down inside the hull of an APC or tank. Not only did it continue to be used for training in the IDF, but it also had a durable life with Israeli special forces and counter-terrorism units that continued into the 21st century. In addition, Uzis proliferated in civilian hands throughout Israel, providing a powerful means of personal security.

[7] Note that unless specifically stated, the term 'Uzi' is often applied in this book as shorthand to include all models of the weapon, not just the standard Uzi model first developed for the IDF

One of the units to keep the Uzi alive in Israeli hands was the *Sayeret Mat'kal*. It was formed in 1957 as an elite reconnaissance and covert operations force, with an emphasis on infiltrating behind enemy lines, or even blending in amongst Arab populations. The covert element of *Sayeret Mat'kal*'s remit naturally meant that it favoured easily concealed weapons such as the Uzi, which could if necessary be hidden beneath baggy clothing or in a small bag.

Sayeret Mat'kal has succeeded in hundreds of high-risk missions over its lifetime, from hostage-rescue actions aboard airliners to targeted assassinations in Arab territories. One of the most famous, Operation *Springtime of Youth*, was delivered in the wake of the Munich massacre of 1972. Led by Ehud Barak, later the Prime Minister of Israel (served 1999–2001), a *Sayeret Mat'kal* unit deployed by speedboat into Beirut on the night of 9/10 April 1973, their mission being to assassinate key PLO/Black September leaders in the city. (There were also secondary targets in the city that night, to be hit by other IDF forces.) To conceal their intentions, they were dressed in gaudy tourist-like clothing; several members of the group were even clothed as women for the sake of authenticity and surprise. Despite their appearance, they were carrying deadly loads: Uzi SMGs, handguns, grenades and explosive charges.

Through bravado and subterfuge, they reached the apartment buildings where the targets were known to be located. They went inside, placed explosive charges against the doors of the relevant apartments, blew the doors in and entered with their Uzis at the ready. One of the men, Muki Betser, here describes what happened when he moved into one of the rooms:

> Finally, the explosion blew open the door in a blast of smoke. I burst
> in with Tzvika, instinctively taking the left-hand turn into the main
> corridor of the apartment, running down the hall I knew so well from
> my drills.

Four strides and I reached my target's office. Half a dozen empty chairs faced the desk. Behind it, filing cabinets reminded me that military intelligence wanted any piece of paper we found. To my right, said the architectural plans I memorized, was the master bedroom door. I swung in that direction, just as the door flew open.

The face I knew from three weeks of carrying his picture in my shirt pocket looked at me as I raised my gun. He slammed the door. Bursts from my Uzi and Tzvika's stitched the bedroom door. I rushed forward and kicked through the remains of the door. [8]

The individual whom Betser was hunting was killed in the bursts of Uzi gunfire, as were the other targets of the raid. Yet the soldiers' – and the Uzis' – work was not done. Just before the operation inside the apartments, a gun battle had erupted outside between security officials and other members of the Israeli team. Betser explained what he experienced as he went out into the street:

[8] The Pedagogic Center, The Department for Jewish Zionist Education, The Jewish Agency for Israel, 1992–2005

I ran down the hall to the stairs, leaping from landing to landing, on our way to the street, where the firefight grew louder. Out the front door, I ducked into the shadow of a tree, scanning the intersection just as a burning Lebanese Land Rover rolled through the intersection. Straight ahead, Amiram Levine in a blonde wig looked like a crazed dancer in the middle of the intersection, his tiny powerful body swinging his Uzi back and forth from target to target. To my right Ehud [Barak] stood in the middle of the intersection doing the same. I added my own fire at the Land Rover, giving Amiram cover for him to run toward me. The Land Rover crashed to a halt against a building. But a second vehicle, a jeep full of reinforcements, came screeching into the box of fire we created at the intersection. Bursts of gunfire knocked the four passengers out of the vehicle, as our fire strafed the jeep.[9]

IDF paratroopers disembark from a Frelon helicopter with their Uzis. Uzis would serve on in some capacity with the IDF until the early years of the 21st century, although in conventional military service the assault rifle became dominant. (Cody Images)

Although the Uzis use a relatively low-powered cartridge, the devastation wrought by their automatic fire is apparent here and in the previous extract, having no problem dealing with doors and vehicle bodywork. Although the *Sayeret Mat'kal* team was small compared to the security forces surrounding them, their Uzis also gave them the ability to generate heavy suppressive firepower. Just two men, working together, were perfectly capable of firing more than 200 rounds in just 30 seconds, although the needs of ammunition conservation would generally prohibit such profligate fire.

[9] Ibid.

Uzi operations such as these have been common in Israel since 1967, but this famous episode illustrates why the Uzi became such a respected tool of the special forces. The development of the Mini, Micro and Pro Uzis has continued the weapon's popularity to this day. It has even been claimed, on the basis of video footage, that IDF soldiers were armed with suppressed Uzis during their boarding operation of a Turkish aid ship bound for Palestine in May 2010, during which nine people were killed. If true – and there is much uncertainty about the event in question – then it demonstrates how the Uzi's format and qualities keep the weapon continually relevant to special forces operations.

While the Uzi has been developed by and for Israel, one unfortunate repercussion of its extremely successful worldwide distribution is that it has also ended up in the hands of Israel's enemies, particularly militant groups – insurgents and terrorists value the Uzi for exactly the same reasons as special forces do. One major supply route for obtaining Uzis is from Iran. During the rule of the Shah of Iran (1941–79), the Iranian armed forces bought thousands of Uzis, but the Islamic revolution in 1979 placed those stocks of weapons into the hands of Israel's enemies, with secondary distribution as far as the armed factions in the West Bank and Gaza Strip. Numerous photographs of militant groups in these and other Arab territories show individuals armed with Uzis, and these weapons have inflicted a not-insignificant death toll on Arab and Israeli alike.

THE UZI ABROAD

The use of the Uzi in non-Israeli hands brings us to the subject of the weapon's spread worldwide. First we will take a look at the world of legitimate military and law-enforcement sales, before moving on to examine the Uzi's place in civilian, and criminal, hands.

Special operator training, Israel, 1980s (opposite)

Here we see two operators from the *Yechida Mishtartit Meyuchedet* (Special Police Unit), otherwise known as *Ya'ma'm*, training with Mini Uzis on a firing range during the 1980s. *Ya'ma'm* was created in 1973–74 as an elite hostage-rescue and assault force within the Israeli National Police Border Guard. The scene depicts a classic 'shoot/don't shoot' range of the type still used today (albeit often with more advanced computer simulations). The cut-out figures represent both threats and harmless civilians, and in this illustration are drawn from actual targets seen in photographs from the time. By including non-stereotypical terrorist figures – such as the woman being peppered by Uzi fire – the firing range forces the operator to make conscious but fast judgements about whether to fire based on actual perceived threats. Both operators are using Mini Uzis. The man in the foreground – an instructor addressing other troopers – has his gun unloaded and stock folded, with a fresh magazine in his left hand. The other man delivers a burst of aimed, controlled fire, targeting all his shots to the centre mass of the torso to ensure an effective take-down. With the Mini Uzi's c. 1,100rpm rate of fire, a half-second burst would be enough to drop most assailants.

It would take almost a book in itself to describe the details of the Uzi's full range of clients. It has been exported to or made under licence in more than 50 countries around the world. The countries who have used or still use the Uzi are as diverse as Algeria, Belgium (manufactured under licence), Brazil, Democratic Republic of Congo, Estonia, Germany (manufactured under licence), Haiti, Italy, Malta, Panama, Peru, Tunisia and the United States.

In the latter, for example, the Uzi was used as a standard SMG of the Secret Service from the 1960s until the 1990s. This became apparent during one of the Uzi's most famous public appearances, on 30 March 1981. The US President, Ronald Reagan, was leaving the Washington Hilton Hotel in Washington, DC, after a speaking engagement. While Reagan headed with his security detail towards his limousine parked outside, a mentally disturbed individual in the crowd, John Hinckley Jr, opened fire on the President with a .22 revolver, discharging all six shots in the chamber. Three of Reagan's entourage were directly shot and wounded, while the President himself was seriously injured by a ricochet. Hinckley was overpowered, but Agent Robert Wanko suddenly pulled out an Uzi from a briefcase and stood guard, watching over the crowd. (Another advantage of the Uzi – it's small enough to place inside a civilian bag, rucksack, briefcase or piece of luggage.) The fear was that the shooting was part of a larger terrorist or gang attack, and that the Uzi might be required to handle multiple targets. As it turned out, the Uzi's magazine remained full that day, but the distinctive profile of the gun was etched more deeply into the public consciousness.

Prior to the Reagan assassination attempt, the Uzi had also hit the headlines in 1974, again in relation to its use by the US Secret Service. This time, the Uzi was the actual cause of danger to the VIP:

> Secretary of State Henry Kissinger narrowly escaped injury Friday when an Israeli made Uzi submachine gun fell from a rack in his plane and discharged two shots. The bullets slightly wounded Secret Service Agent Walter Bothe in the right arm and grazed his forehead. Kissinger was about 20 feet away when the incident occurred, as his plane was taxiing for take-off from Cairo bound for Damascus, and he was not hurt. Later he was able to joke about the incident with Bothe and reporters. Bothe remained with the party ...
>
> Security officials said they kept the Uzi gun on hand in case crowds got out of control. When it discharged accidentally, Bothe fell to the floor in the galley of the plane and Kissinger was rushed to his forward cabin by other Secret Service agents.
>
> Bothe was given medical attention aboard the plane. Departure was delayed 30 minutes while agents checked the craft. They found one bullet hole in the ceiling and patched it.[10]

[10] *The Milwaukee Journal*, 11 October 1974

Two things are notable about this incident. The first is the intended use of the Uzi by the Secret Service – 'in case crowds got out of control'. While other Secret Service weapons, such as sniper rifles and handguns, would be for specific individual targets, the Uzi is presented as a close-quarters area weapon, selected specifically for its ability to suppress and break up large bodies of people in dire situations. The other interesting point is that the Uzi had an accidental discharge. As discussed above in the section on the Uzi's operation, the Uzi has a total of three safety systems in play, so the chances of it going off without a hand around the grip and pulling the trigger are extremely low, and the circumstances must have been unusual indeed.

Certainly, the Secret Service themselves do not appear to have had any lack of confidence in the Uzi following this incident. Nearly 20 years later, in July 1991, a different President – George H. W. Bush – made a public visit to the Secret Service's training ground in rural Maryland, where he was given a guided tour of both the facilities and the weaponry. Journalists were also given an insight into Secret Service firepower:

Probably the most famous photograph of an Uzi – Special Agent Robert Wanko stands guard with an Uzi during the attempted assassination of President Ronald Reagan on 30 March 1981. The gun had been held ready in a briefcase. (Getty Images)

49

Secret Service spokesman Robert Snow ... escorted reporters to the firing range where they were briefed on the Secret Service weapons and were taught to shoot one of them, an Uzi submachine gun. The Secret Service prefers the Uzi because of its triple safety system and because it was simple and accurate, reporters were told.[11]

Obviously by the 1990s, with many more weapons options on the market, the Secret Service still preferred the Uzi, and questions about its safety were not an issue.

Away, for the moment, from the United States, the other prominent military and police users of the Uzi have included the Irish Gardaí police, Sri Lanka's Police Special Task Force (in addition to army and navy units) and the German Bundeswehr, which adopted the Uzi as the MP2 in 1959. The Uzi found a new vein of foreign sales during the 1970s amongst recently created counter-terrorist forces, of which there was a global increase during this most troubled of decades. The Netherlands, for example, adopted the Uzi for the *Bijzondere Bijstands Eenheid* (BBE), the elite Dutch counter-terrorist force created from the ranks of the equally professional Royal Netherlands Marine Corps (RNLMC). The BBE's most famous action came in May 1977, when nine South Moluccan terrorists took a train and its 97 passengers hostage, while four other terrorists held 105 children and four teachers prisoner at a Bovensmilde schoolhouse. Both incidents were resolved by force, but while the school was liberated without bloodshed, rescuing the train hostages was a far more violent affair. Following a fast, low-level pass by two Dutch Starfighter jets over the roof of the train – to disorientate and confuse the terrorists – BBE troopers, many wielding Uzis, burst through the doors of the train and proceeded to take it back. Six of the nine terrorists were killed in the action; two hostages also died in the incident.

Another incident in which the Uzi excelled was in Lima, Peru, on 17 December 1996, when 14 terrorists from the Túpac Amaru Revolutionary Movement (MRTA) took hundreds of officials hostage at the Japanese ambassador's residence. Although many of the hostages were quickly released, 72 were kept captive in a siege situation that ran on until 22 April 1997. On that day, in an operation planned in cooperation with the British SAS, Peruvian commandos armed with Mini Uzis stormed the residence following a series of three well-timed explosions, which in themselves killed many of the terrorists. The 140 commandos then embarked on a 40-minute close-quarters gun battle with their

A Dutch Army soldier cradles his Uzi. Just using the standard iron sights, the Uzi could deliver fire convincingly over ranges of 100–200m, after which assault rifles were more persuasive. (Cody Images)

[11] *The Deseret News*, 6 July 1991

adversaries. Although the terrorists themselves were heavily armed with automatic weaponry, they were no match for either the tactics or the combined firepower of the raiders; all 14 terrorists were killed, including at least three who were executed after being captured.

From the 1990s onwards, the Uzi has been replaced in many quarters by carbines such as the US M4 and submachine guns like the Heckler & Koch MP5 (see the 'Impact' chapter for more discussion of comparable weapons), but it has never entirely fallen out of service with professional military units. Its service with law enforcement has been somewhat more controversial, however.

Uzis have been distributed widely throughout Latin America either as imports or via licensed production. Here we see a Honduran Air Force security soldier holding an Uzi; unfortunately, many Uzis in the region have gone into criminal hands. (Cody Images)

Uzis in American law enforcement

US law enforcement forms a fascinating case study in our history of the Uzi. Imports of Uzis into the United States for law-enforcement use began in the 1960s, but it was in the 1970s and '80s that Uzi sales to this specific market really accelerated. There were two, interrelated factors behind this rise. The first was the creation of the nation's Special Weapons and Tactics (SWAT) units, initially established by the Los Angeles Police Department (LAPD) in 1968–69, in the aftermath of the city's 1965 Watts Riots. The SWAT teams multiplied until most urban US police departments had one at their disposal, and they had access to all manner of hi-tech and powerful weaponry, including SMGs.

The birth of the SWAT teams encouraged (although was not entirely responsible for) the second important effect that encouraged law-enforcement Uzi sales in the United States. This is what can be called the progressive 'militarization' of the police. The 1970s and '80s in particular were a time in which the American criminal community seemed to be upgunning itself with assault rifles and various SMGs, especially in the context of gang and drug crime. In response, many regular police departments put its officers through SWAT-style training – by April 1975 some 467 police departments had undergone such instruction under a Federal Bureau of Investigation (FBI) programme run at the US Marine Corps military base in Quantico, Virginia. At the same time, even isolated rural police departments with notably low levels of crime began to look into kitting themselves out to compete with the criminals.

For many, this upgunning process involved getting Uzis. One 1970s report into police departments operating in placid, low-population suburbs of the San Francisco Bay area found that the departments had established SWAT-style teams armed with Uzis, alongside handguns fitted with silencers and hunting knives strapped in scabbards to their chests. They had even discussed the possibility of purchasing a helicopter gunship.

In part, the desire for increased firepower on the streets was justified by some major city incidents in which heavily armed criminals – including those armed with Uzis – managed to hold off less well armed police for prolonged periods while inflicting heavy casualties. Yet for some police departments, tooling up with heavy firepower – but without adequate training – resulted in serious legal and ethical problems. The disquiet amongst many officials for this trend emerges in an article in the *New York Times* in 1989:

Suburb Wants an Uzi for Every Officer
WINNETKA, Ill. July 8—Police officials in this affluent lakefront suburb of Chicago are considering something even their beleaguered colleagues in Detroit or Washington have not done: equipping their regular police patrols with Uzi submachine guns that can fire up to ten rounds a second and are a favorite of military commando units. [...] Several criminal justice experts described the Winnetka plan as the most exotic example of a growing trend among police departments around the country to acquire more powerful and deadly firepower of their own to compete with criminals and drug dealers who themselves are better armed. [...]

Chief Timm [the Chief of Police in Winnetka] wants to use the Uzis to replace the department's arsenal of aging shotguns, which are ordinarily carried as a backup inside patrol cars. He is also asking the village to replace the department's standard issue sidearms, .38-caliber Smith and Wesson revolvers that carry 6 bullets, with Glock 17s, an Austrian-made semiautomatic pistol that carries a magazine of 18 bullets.[12]

The article goes on to quote several legal experts deeply worried about the police's desire to equip themselves with Uzis or similar weapons. Concern was felt especially in areas that had virtually zero serious armed crime and in which officers had scant experience of drawing their firearms in anger.

An example of what could happen when police actually deployed Uzis was seen north of the US border, in Canada. Canadian law enforcement also succumbed to the militarization urge, although to a lesser extent than the United States. In one incident in 1989, Uzi-armed officers from Sherbrooke, Quebec, discovered to their detriment the sheer power of the Uzi:

Witnesses say Police just Opened Fire
SHERBROOKE, Que. (CP) – Sherbrooke police sprayed bullets through the locked door of a motel room with a rapid-fire Uzi submachine-gun before ordering the occupants to surrender, witnesses have told a coroner's inquest into the killing of an innocent man in the police raid.

Civilians and policemen testified Monday that 21 bullets were fired as officers stormed the motel room in nearby Rock Forest on Dec. 23

[12] William E. Schmidt, *New York Times* 9 July 1989

An Israeli-manufactured Uzi Carbine, easily distinguished by the long barrel. Such weapons became the centre of vigorous debate about which guns were prohibited under the US Federal Assault Weapons Ban of 1994. (Time & Life Pictures/Getty Images)

in the hope of catching the killers of a Brink's guard during a robbery here the day before. 'We wanted to take them by surprise,' one Sherbrooke policemen, Sgt. Roger Cloutler, told a standing-room-only audience on the first day of the inquest into the death of Serge Beaudoin, 33.[13]

During the storming of the motel room, the Uzi was fired several times on full-auto mode. Jean-Paul Beaumon, a workmate of the deceased, was woken by the roar of SMG fire and was also struck by a 9mm round, which miraculously went into his chin and emerged from near his ear without causing life-threatening injuries. His friend was not so lucky. He was hit by no fewer than eight rounds, including one that penetrated his heart and killed him in the motel corridor. The death toll could have been worse. Edward Redden, another guest in the motel, was sleeping in an adjoining room with his wife when he was startled awake:

> Redden said there was some commotion in the motel's interior and then what sounded like 'the burst of a machine-gun or a jackhammer. I pushed my wife off the side of the bed. Then I went over myself,' he recalled. Five bullets penetrated the wall into the room, with one lodging in the wall just seven centimetres above his pillow.[14]

In such civilian settings, the military capabilities of the Uzi seem frighteningly inappropriate. Yet as countless elite units have proven, the Uzi delivers *controllable* firepower in *well-trained* hands.

CIVILIAN UZIS

We should remind ourselves that in many countries civilian Uzi ownership is perfectly legal, although there are naturally wide variations in ease of purchase, conditions of use and weapon configuration. In certain war-torn African states, for example, Uzis are available simply if you have the bundle of dollars to purchase them (typically around $500). In the UK,

[13] *The Leader Post*, 14 February 1984
[14] Ibid.

by contrast, the only Uzi available to you will be a deactivated one, with (according to 1995 standards of deactivation) its barrel cut and its action welded solid, rendering it completely unable to fire. (Trying to obtain a 'live' Uzi will result in a minimum five-year prison sentence.)

In the United States, the place where the Uzi has been most associated with gangland crime (at least in popular Western culture), the picture is complicated by myth and numerous federal and state gun laws. In general terms, since the early 1980s, civilians in the United States have been able to buy some version of the Uzi, either full-auto or semi-auto, and produced by either IMI or US-based licensed producers.

There is no doubting the sheer popularity of the Uzi when it first went on sale to the mass market in the United States, despite the disquiet of many about the potential of the weapon. Both the questions and the enthusiasms come through clearly in the following newspaper article:

Gun Dealer Sells Israeli Uzis

A gun dealer selling 200 Israeli-made Uzi submachine guns he calls the 'ultimate weapon' said his store had a 'lot of customers' when the gun went on sale for the first time Monday. But police are protesting the sale of the guns, modified to be semi-automatic and apparently legal to sell. Law-enforcement officials figure the guns will wind up in the hands of criminals, perhaps drug smugglers.

'Who else is going to buy them?' asked Det. Gus Ewell of the Dade County police. 'A sportsman is not going to buy a gun like this for hunting.'

Tony Senatore, who figures the sale of the Uzi will help promote the gun shop he opened in Miramar seven months ago, advertised his guns Sunday for $598 each. He said his is the first dealership in the United States to sell the Uzi without restrictions, and he said the guns are being purchased by gun collectors.

'Who's buying the guns? Normal people,' Senatore said. 'It's a collector's item. People collect military items. This happens to be the ultimate military weapon. So many people are coming in here today I'm going crazy.'

Senatore said orders will be delivered March 15 in a 'molded Styrofoam case, complete with carrying sling.' He said he's getting the guns from Southern Gun Distributors of Miami.

Ewell says one or two gun collectors may buy the Uzi 'and a couple of hunting nuts. The rest are going to show up in homicide and drug ripoffs.' [15]

On the one hand, we have the view that the Uzis are simply historically significant firearms that will appeal to collectors; on the other hand, the critics see the Uzi as having no practical purpose in civilian hands, other than to become a weapon of choice for murderers and gang members. Such debates about all military-type firearms persist to this day.

[15] *Sarasota Herald Tribune*, 12 February 1980

The legal context in which the Uzi has existed and thrived in the United States revolves around major pieces of 20th-century firearms legislation, principally the National Firearms Act of 1934; the Gun Control Act of 1968; the Firearm Owners Protection Act of 1986; and the Federal Assault Weapons Ban of 1994. Unpacking these complicated pieces of legislation in detail is impossible here, but an overview of key points is useful for understanding how the Uzi has fitted into American gun culture.

The National Firearms Act of 1934 was framed during a violent time in American history, when the rise of gangster violence, committed with tools such as the Thompson M1928 submachine gun, led Congress to attempt to restrict access to firepower without infringing Second Amendment rights too heavily. The 'NFA' weapons subject to the legislation include 'machine guns' (actually any weapon capable of firing more than one cartridge per trigger pull), short-barrelled rifles or shotguns (i.e. concealable long guns), suppressors in general and, in the Act's current form, a variety of other lethal devices that could be put to nefarious purposes. Note that the Act does not prohibit the ownership of full-auto firearms (what are known as Class 3 weapons), but those wishing to own such guns must buy them from a registered Class 3 dealer, receive approval of ownership by local law-enforcement agencies and pay an additional tax for ownership (at the time of writing, $200). If the individual can tick all these boxes, then a full-auto firearm can be theirs. Although cast a long time ago, the NFA is still a major work of law governing access to firearms in the United States.

Uzis have had a wide distribution throughout the African continent, in civilian as well as official hands, and as both imports and through licensed manufacture. Here a plain-clothes policeman carries an Uzi-based submachine gun while guarding a refugee camp in Darfur, 2004. (Jim Watson/AFP/Getty Images)

There are numerous accessories for the Uzi-series weapons, including this IWI thigh holster for the Micro Uzi. Worn like this under a long coat, the weapon would be perfectly concealed from view. (Israel Weapon Industries)

More recently, the Gun Control Act of 1968 focused not on the types of weapons sold, but more on how and to whom they could be sold. The Act prohibited the interstate transfer of guns between private individuals, placed restrictions on the type of person who could buy a firearm (such as felons and those under court orders), and made various other social measures. Until 1986, these two acts in themselves made the purchase of an Uzi open to all those of clean character and the financial means, state legislation depending. In 1986, however, the Firearm Owners Protection Act, while actually loosening many of the restrictions put in place by the 1968 laws (including interstate transfers), actually banned the sale of full-auto weapons manufactured after the date of enactment, except to military or law-enforcement personnel.

Unlike the previous Acts, this piece of legislation did have a major impact on Uzi ownership. Because full-auto Uzis manufactured *before* 1986 were still legal and transferable, but the stock within the United States was now effectively limited, the prices of full-auto variants climbed significantly. Today, the prices have reached wallet-stretching levels, the costs proving a de facto limitation on the legal ownership of such weapons. For example, a browse on the internet for current (2011) Uzi sales reveals such gems as an IMI Mini Uzi, complete with original box and papers and in good condition, retailing at $8,999.99. (A standard Uzi on the same website was selling for an identical price.) To understand how much the full-auto legislation adds to the price tag, consider that another website was selling a brand-new semi-auto Vector Arms Uzi Carbine for just $845.00.

In 1994, another piece of major firearms legislation was passed that switched the focus from full-auto to semi-auto weapons. The Federal Assault Weapons Ban (AWB) was passed by a government attempting to tackle what it saw as the unacceptable availability of military-style weaponry to the populace, fuelling high levels of gun-related crime. The legislation targeted what it called 'assault weapons', the definition of which was spelt out at length, and is worth quoting in detail for our subsequent analysis:

(b) DEFINITION OF SEMIAUTOMATIC ASSAULT WEAPON –
Section 921(a) of title 18, United States Code, is amended by adding at
the end the following new paragraph:

(30) The term 'semiautomatic assault weapon' means—

  (A) any of the firearms, or copies or duplicates of the firearms in any
     caliber, known as –
   (i) Norinco, Mitchell, and Poly Technologies Avtomat Kalashnikovs
     (all models);
   (ii) Action Arms Israeli Military Industries UZI and Galil;
  (iii) Beretta Ar70 (SC-70);
  (iv) Colt AR-15;
   (v) Fabrique National FN/FAL, FN/LAR, and FNC;
  (vi) SWD M-10, M-11, M-11/9, and M-12;
 (vii) Steyr AUG;
(viii) INTRATEC TEC-9, TEC-DC9 and TEC-22; and
  (ix) revolving cylinder shotguns, such as (or similar to) the Street
     Sweeper and Striker 12;

  (B) a semiautomatic rifle that has an ability to accept a detachable
     magazine and has at least 2 of –
   (i) a folding or telescoping stock;
   (ii) a pistol grip that protrudes conspicuously beneath the action of
     the weapon;
  (iii) a bayonet mount;
  (iv) a flash suppressor or threaded barrel designed to accommodate
     a flash suppressor; and
   (v) a grenade launcher;

  (C) a semiautomatic pistol that has an ability to accept a detachable
     magazine and has at least 2 of –
   (i) an ammunition magazine that attaches to the pistol outside of
     the pistol grip;
   (ii) a threaded barrel capable of accepting a barrel extender, flash
     suppressor, forward handgrip, or silencer;
  (iii) a shroud that is attached to, or partially or completely encircles,
     the barrel and that permits the shooter to hold the firearm with
     the nontrigger hand without being burned;
  (iv) a manufactured weight of 50 ounces or more when the pistol is
     unloaded; and
   (v) a semiautomatic version of an automatic firearm; and

  (D) a semiautomatic shotgun that has at least 2 of –
   (i) a folding or telescoping stock;
   (ii) a pistol grip that protrudes conspicuously beneath the action of
     the weapon;
  (iii) a fixed magazine capacity in excess of 5 rounds; and
  (iv) an ability to accept a detachable magazine.

The 1994 Federal Assault Weapon Ban expired in 2004, prompting vigorous debate in the United States between pro- and anti-gun lobbies. Here Senator Frank R. Lautenberg (Democrat, New Jersey) holds a plastic toy Uzi Carbine to illustrate his point in the debate. (Congressional Quarterly/Getty Images)

For many in the US gun community, the broad scope of what constituted an 'assault weapon' raised eyebrows. As we can see from the list at the beginning of this quotation, the Uzi was categorized along with weapons of entirely different classes, such as the FN FAL rifle and the Steyr AUG. Yet on almost all counts, except 'an ammunition magazine that attaches to the pistol outside of the pistol grip', the Uzi ticked all the boxes of what qualified as a federally defined assault weapon.

Note that in a similar way to the Firearm Owners Protection Act of 1986, the AWB did not make illegal the ownership of 'assault weapons' manufactured before the AWB's enactment, only the subsequent domestic manufacture and sale of such weapons for the civilian market, or their importation.

Various approaches were taken to circumvent the legislation. Low-capacity magazines were one option, but the clause about the 'pistol grip that protrudes conspicuously beneath the action of the weapon' posed a significant challenge for a weapon like the Uzi. The solution offered by the Chinese Norinco company was to make unlicensed copies of the Uzi Model B Carbine (it had begun to do so in 1990) adapted with a large wooden 'thumbhole' stock. This was a one-piece unit that attached to the rear of the weapon's receiver and formed the grip, but with a long wooden extension reaching back from the base of the pistol grip to the underside of the stock. The barrel was welded into place to prevent its removal (and therefore its modification or replacement). There was no bayonet lug and the magazine capacity was limited to just ten rounds.

IMI produced a similarly modified version known as the 'Uzi Sporter', imported into the United States in 1997 via Uzi America – a subsidiary of the Mossberg firearms company, with consequent controversy (see below). Although the 'sporterized' approach was visually displeasing, in many cases it altered the profile of the gun in an attempt, not always successful, to help it escape the pistol grip clauses of the AWB.

The AWB was signed into law for a period of ten years, and in 2004, under the presidency of George W. Bush, it lapsed and to date has not been renewed, despite several attempts to do so. For this reason, new manufactured semi-auto Uzis are back on the market in the United States, manufactured by companies such as Vector Arms, who produce the guns in 9mm, .45 ACP and .22 LR. The Vector models include standard and Mini Uzis, both of which can be bought with regular or carbine barrels, and fixed, folding or side-folding stocks. For those wanting a more sophisticated version of the Uzi, Vector also manufactures stainless steel versions, with the sights and the sides of the receiver made of the brighter metal.

The upshot of all the legislation in effect at the time of writing, and looking simply at a federal level, is that ownership of full-auto and semi-auto Uzis is still possible for civilians, as long as they comply with the various statutes and that the purchaser jumps through all the relevant hoops to buy one. State legislation, however, dramatically muddies the waters, as there are many states that prohibit ownership of full-auto weapons completely, and others with very strict regulations on the possession of 'assault weapons'. The idea that anyone in the United States can walk into a gun shop and buy an Uzi is largely a media myth.

A criminologist at the Criminology Laboratory in Ciudad Juarez, north Mexico, displays an Uzi seized by local police. This Uzi was part of a haul of weapons used by local drug traffickers, and when this photograph was taken, 28 May 2008, there had been 1,378 violent gang-related deaths in Mexico so far that year. (Alfredo Estella/AFP/Getty Images)

UZIS IN CRIME

In Bogota, Colombia, in the early hours of Saturday 24 June 2000, nightclubbers were enjoying themselves at the Reminencias nightclub in the San Jorge neighbourhood. The area of the city was known for its tough living and gangland violence, but most hoped for nothing more than an evening of fun. At one point an argument broke out between a woman and three men – the woman was rejecting requests for a dance. After a heated exchange of words, the three men left the nightclub, and normality seemed to resume.

Several minutes later, the men returned, one of them gripping an Uzi. It can't have been difficult to obtain. Colombia has purchased thousands of Uzis over the decades, many of which have ended up illegally channelled into gangland. The Uzi-armed man walked into the midst of the nightclubbers, and opened fire on full-auto, indiscriminately scything down any individuals who were in his sights. By the time he stopped shooting, 11 people were dead and seven wounded.

This incident is exceptional, but it is not unprecedented for Uzis to have been used in some of history's worst civilian massacres. In the United States on 18 July 1984, deranged gunman James Oliver Huberty marched into a McDonald's restaurant in the San Ysidro area of San Diego, California, armed to the teeth and intent on venting murderous impulses. His arsenal that day consisted of a Winchester 12-gauge pump-action shotgun, a 9mm Browning Hi-Power handgun and also a civilian-version Uzi semi-automatic, which offered the greatest firepower in his collection. Huberty embarked on a 77-minute killing spree, in which he fired 257 rounds of ammunition, most of them from his Uzi. In total he was able to kill 21 people and wound 19 others. He was finally brought down by a single shot from a SWAT team sniper, Chuck Foster, who noted that Huberty was striding around with his Uzi seconds before the rifle bullet killed him.

Such stories are shocking, and remind us of what can occur when powerful weapons such as the Uzi fall into the wrong hands. For it is the case that much of the notoriety of the Uzi comes not from its use in military hands, nor from the enjoyment of thousands of law-abiding Uzi owners, who own the gun for no more sinister a purpose than punching paper targets full of holes. Yet it is an undoubted fact that large numbers of Uzis in the civilian world have made their way into criminal hands, and have taken many lives in the process.

In the discussion of illegally acquired and applied Uzis, we have to be careful to separate hype from reality, particularly as the Uzi has garnered such a prominent profile in films, TV and the press. For all the Uzi's high visibility, in most societies firearms crimes are overwhelmingly committed by individuals with cheap handguns, which are perfectly concealable and don't come with the hefty price tag often attached to an SMG. In the United States, for example, a survey in 1997 found that 15 per cent of state prison inmates and 13 per cent of federal prison inmates were carrying a handgun during the crime that resulted in their incarceration. In both cases, by contrast, only 2 per cent carried any sort of what the report labelled as 'military style semi-automatic guns'. From the 1970s to the present day, illegally acquired Uzis have contributed fractionally to overall firearms crime.

Such a truth is often overridden in the public mind by the fact than when an Uzi is used for criminal violence, the consequences can be so appalling. On 30 August 1987, for example, 23-year-old Minh Le, a Vietnamese immigrant, was confronted by his family over some money missing from his aunt's bank account. Fearing a 'loss of face' over the incident, Le decided to respond by pulling out a semi-auto Uzi and opening fire on his relatives. Before he turned the gun on himself, Le killed a total of five people, all but one directly related to him. The case proved to be contentious legally. The Uzi used in the crime had been acquired perfectly legitimately, Le taking advantage of a special permit system issued by the Massachusetts Department of Public Safety.

Yet crimes equal to or far greater than this have been committed with guns other than Uzis. Two years later, for instance, drifter Patrick Purdy walked into Cleveland Elementary School in Stockton, California, and opened fire on the pupils and teachers with an AK-47, killing five children and one teacher and wounding another 29 children. In the UK on 19 August 1987, one Michael Ryan, similarly armed to Purdy, killed 16 people and wounded 15 others in the town of Hungerford, Berkshire. Seen in context, the Uzi has no special claim to criminal lethality.

More than anything, what associated the Uzi with criminal use was its apparent prominence during the US gang wars of the 1970s, '80s and '90s. Certainly, by the beginning of the 1980s the levels of gun violence in the United States had reached epidemic proportions. African-American and Latino gangs, such as the infamous Crips and Bloods of Los Angeles, and various motorbike and extremist groups, began to expand throughout the

Uzi in gangland. Two men in Brooklyn, New York, 1988, sit on the steps of a housing project, one of them cradling an Uzi. The Uzi became something of a status symbol within US gang culture during this period. (Getty Images)

United States, fuelled by crack cocaine and (for some) a variety of rap music that frequently eulogized killing. The violence was all too real – in 1979 the total numbers of homicides in the United States was 13,582, but by 1993 the death toll had escalated to 17,083, having climbed inexorably during the 1980s. For gang members living in a world of casual death and 'drive-by shootings', weapons such as the AK-47, Uzi and MAC-10 became popular force multipliers.

The US media feasted on seemingly constant stories about firefights and violence that seemed more at home in a war zone. On 22 July 1991, for example, a four-year-old girl was killed and three others wounded (including the girl's pregnant mother) in Harlem, New York, when two men sprayed the street with automatic gunfire from a passing car. Despite the fact that around 80 per cent of all guns used in criminal activity were bought through illegal markets, America began to look long and hard at the guns it was legitimately importing and buying.

In 1997, a controversy hit the headlines when the aforementioned Uzi America received a permit to import 'sporterized' Uzis and Galil rifles. It was far from the only company importing such weapons at the time, but its place in the political landscape was unique, as journalist Marilyn Henry noted in the 16 November *Jerusalem Post*:

> Although the number is small, the Uzi is the fear-inspiring symbol in US gun-control debates.
>
> 'The Uzi has gotten a reputation that you can't do anything about,' said Aharon Kleiman of Tel Aviv University's Jaffee Center for Strategic Studies. 'It has negative name recognition. It is a good and effective and multipurpose (weapon) that is associated with crime, assassinations and gang wars.'
>
> Gun-control lobbyists were frightened that it had become a 'fashion statement,' said Bob Walker, president of Handgun Control, an anti-gun lobbying group. 'Many gangs are going to buy it just for the name,' he said. 'It's a symbol of power.'

Special forces have naturally been attracted to the Micro Uzi's scaled-down size and scaled-up firepower. Here a marine of the Peruvian armed forces trains with a Micro Uzi during tactical manoeuvres. (Cody Images)

This Irish Garda tactical officer has mounted a flashlight to the muzzle of his Uzi. In low-light conditions, accurate snap-shooting can be performed simply by illuminating the target with the torch and pulling the trigger. (Israel Weapon Industries)

Jonathan Mossberg, president of Uzi America, disagreed. 'I don't think this is the kind of weapon that the gangs will go for,' he said. 'We are three to four times more expensive than other semi-automatics.'

Although the Uzi was by no means top of US imports in the civilian weapons market, President Bill Clinton became personally involved with the industry row. In a radio address he firmly stated that 'We've banned these guns because you don't need an Uzi to go deer hunting, and everyone knows it.' The US federal administration therefore sought a prohibition on the imports, which would effectively prevent 10,000 Uzis, alongside up to a million other weapons, from entering the country over a 3–4 year period.

To beef up the government's actions, Senator Dianne Feinstein directly approached the Israeli government of Prime Minister Benjamin Netanyahu, who bowed to US pressure and announced a suspension of IMI small-arms exports to the United States for a duration of three months, which extended into a longer period under ongoing US pressure.

As we have seen, the Uzi has been a cause of both fear and controversy since its inception, and it keeps making occasional appearances in the headlines. In the UK, a country with some of the most restrictive gun laws in the world, there have been recent headlines about deactivated or replica Uzis being converted into live weapons in illegal backstreet workshops. In the UK, pre-1995 deactivations were less extensive than those done to

A Palestinian gunman displays his Uzi during the funeral of a comrade killed during clashes with Israeli troops in Hebron in October 2000. Uzis have entered Arab service via weapons captured from Israeli forces and from stocks formerly held by pre-revolutionary Iran. (Getty Images)

post-1995 standards, the earlier guns retaining their internal parts so they could be cocked and dry-fired. Some of these weapons were indeed restored to working order by criminals. In March 2004, William Greenwood, 76, and his son Mitchell, 42, from South Wingfield, Derbyshire, were convicted of manufacturing illegal firearms and selling them to the criminal community, each man receiving a seven-year prison sentence. More than 700 deactivated firearms, and many reactivated weapons, were recovered from the two men's home, including numerous Uzis. The simplicity of the Uzi – one of its crowning virtues in military use – does make it suitable in some cases for reactivations. In many instances, however, there has also been hysteria fed by poor understanding of the law and of the difficulties (sometimes impossibility) of converting deactivated firearms back into full working models. Homes and businesses of legitimate traders have been raided, only for the police to have been quoted the law back at them, and had to go back to the station empty-handed. Uzis therefore remain a popular seller in the UK deactivated market, owned by a wide range of people, from gun enthusiasts to historians wanting to own a piece of firearms history.

IMPACT
Competitors and culture

During the 1980s, the BBC's Radio 1 show 'Steve Wright in the Afternoon' contained a short jingle, just a few seconds long, in which a voice impersonating Arnold Schwarzenegger suddenly intoned the words 'Uzi 9mm!' with the famous robot-like menace. The lines come from the film *The Terminator* (1984), in which the cyborg assassin played by Schwarzenegger visits a gun shop to get tooled up for his mission – to kill Sarah Connor. Because of both the jingle and the film, the words 'Uzi 9mm' became a catchphrase of my teenage years. The words were even cast into a dance tune.

In the context of the times, when the Uzi was already gaining some notoriety, such cultural references gave the Uzi intense imaginative cachet. Relatively few weapons in history become true household names amongst the broad sweep of the general population, but the Uzi surely must rank alongside the Spitfire, AK-47 and the 'Scud' missile as one of the most high-profile pieces of military kit in history.

Journalists and writers have also treated the Uzi with a certain amount of reverence, often derived from a lack of experience of firearms and from the narratives that have attached themselves to the weapon. In the following extract from a *New York Times* column of 27 December 1992, the journalist is taken to a firing range 'to learn more about the guns that are at the centre of public debates over arming police and disarming criminals':

> Now Stan [the firearms instructor] produces two fearsome assault weapons. One is an Israeli-made Uzi submachine gun, the other an American-made Tec-9 manufactured for single shots but illegally altered to fire as an automatic.

> The Uzi feels substantial and appears well suited for military use. Its moderate rate of fire makes it possible to keep the barrel under control as recoil forces it up. The Tec-9, a shoddier item, fires a terrifying 750 shots per minute. The barrel swings wildly as I attempt to keep it down.

Although the journalist possibly has little prior knowledge of firearms, he judiciously distinguishes between the Uzi's military-grade quality and the feel of the Tec-9. He is obviously also given proper instruction in how to hold and fire the weapon, keeping control of its muzzle climb throughout a full-auto burst. What is apparent is that both the journalist and, obviously, the paper that commissioned the story, are fascinated at getting to something like the reality of these infamous weapons.

As our extended journey through the history of the Uzi SMG has at times shown, distinguishing the reality of the Uzi from the truth is not always straightforward, often because the mystique that it has accrued in the hands of special forces soldiers and criminals has distracted from the original purpose and integrity of its design. Matters have also been clouded by the Uzi's frequent appearances at the movies.

THE CULTURAL UZI

We have already noted one cinematic instance that pushed the Uzi deep into the public imagination. Yet *The Terminator* is far from the only film in which the Uzi has taken centre stage. The list of films in which it has starred are numerous: Mel Gibson clutched one in *Air America* (1990); numerous movie posters featuring Chuck Norris show him posturing with one or two Uzis, such as that for *Delta Force 2* (1990); and several villainous characters in the *Lethal Weapon* series had Uzis as their weapon of choice. But Uzis were shown in a rather more realistic light in Steven Spielberg's film *Munich* (2005), which includes a depiction of the *Springtime of Youth* operation described above.

'You know your weapons, buddy.' The Uzi's appearance in *The Terminator* sealed its status as the world's most famous submachine gun. (Orion/The Kobal Collection)

Such visual expositions of the Uzi aren't always given to realism. Terrorists seem to fire the Uzi with total disregard for ammunition consumption, rattling through dozens of rounds without the need to reload. The postures in which the guns are wielded can also stretch credence, with Uzis gripped at bizarre angles at the end of fully outstretched arms and fired on full-auto. Many of these representations haven't educated the public about the reality of the Uzi, but they have made it instantly recognizable.

The Uzi's cultural presence isn't limited to moving images only. Several artists have depicted Uzis in their work, attempting to demonstrate how an iconic weapon can be treated purely on the basis of its aesthetics, its actual purpose remaining as a silent threat in the background. Michael Tompsett's 'Uzi Sub Machine Gun on Purple', for example, is a work of pure pop art, three stylized Uzis stacked on top of each other in contrasting colours and angles. Tompsett has further explored the weapon in his 'Mini Uzi Submachine Gun on Green'. While such artworks are by no means intended to act as studies of the weapon's technical attributes, they do remind us of the proportionality and balance that makes the Uzi such a fine weapon to handle.

In the world of music, the Uzi's contribution has been far less delicate. Along with the AK-47 and MAC-10, the Uzi featured in many 'gangsta rap' lyrics during the 1980s and 1990s. Some of these lyrics lauded the Uzi as a settler of scores and giver of respect on the tough streets of New York or Los Angeles. The group Public Enemy, for example, released a track entitled 'My Uzi Weighs a Ton' during the 1990s, which placed the Uzi at the heart of gangland culture, with lyrics such as 'I'll show you my gun – my Uzi weighs a ton/Because I'm Public Enemy number one.'

Such lyrics and depictions did little to endear the Uzi to many US lawmakers, police leaders and government officials. The Uzi was designed by military professionals for use by military professionals, but the gangsta rap movement presented it as an easy route to respect on the street, a fatalistic icon of violent lives. At a cultural level, therefore, the Uzi SMG has had about as much influence as any weapon can hope to achieve, although the representations have not always done the gun justice.

THE UZI COMPARED

Judging the impact of the Uzi on its merits alone gives us only part of the equation. To assess its importance properly, we must also hold it up to the weapons against which it has competed, both on the battlefield and for sales. Three such firearms stand out as salient – the AK-47, the Ingram MAC-10 and the Heckler & Koch MP5 – and a comparative look at their properties further illuminates the Uzi's.

We have already touched on the Uzi's relationship to the AK-47 in the context of the Six-Day War, and the events that led to the Uzi's replacement in regular IDF service by the Galil. In general terms of usability, and using 'AK-47' to denote all Kalashnikov variants, there is actually little to separate the Uzi and the AK-47. Both are easy to fire and maintain, deliver heavy automatic firepower and are rugged in the field. In the AK's case, that ruggedness is even more legendary than that of the Uzi. Alan James, the Rhodesian African Rifles soldier mentioned previously, discovered just how reliable the AK could be along the banks of the Zambezi river:

> On the Zambesi River, they [enemy insurgents] had a river crossing from Zambia. They came across in dinghies, and we had a contact with them as they hit the shoreline. Lots of them went into the water with their packs and all the rest of it, most of them couldn't swim ... but once the contact was over anything that was lost in the river obviously you couldn't see or retrieve it. Six months later we were coming along that same stretch of river – remember it was the dry season – and we saw the butt of an AK-47 sticking out of the sand ... still in the water. We pulled it out and the magazine was still in it. It was on 'Fire' and was actually on automatic. We got the magazine out, but we couldn't clear the breech. We tried to kick it ... we kicked it several times but it was solid. So we put the magazine back in and pulled the trigger and it fired all 30 rounds.

Such a level of reliability would be beyond even the standards of the Uzi. Combined with one of the greatest distribution success stories in history, the AK-47 went on to levels of international use that surpassed the Uzi at least eightfold. An estimated 80 million, but possibly as many as 100 million, AK-type rifles have been distributed around the world since the late 1940s, and they have reshaped the security map of our planet – not for the better.

The Uzi was outstripped by the AK-47 because the Soviet weapon perfectly represented the shift into the era of the assault rifle, whereas the heyday of the SMG type was really during World War II. (We mustn't also

US troops familiarize themselves with an AK-47-type weapon. The AK-47 revolutionized small-arms distribution during the second half of the 20th century, and its appearance during the Six-Day War forced the IDF to re-evaluate the Uzi. (US Department of Defense)

forget that the AK-47 also became stunningly cheap.) The heart of this shift was as much about ammunition as about the gun that fired it. The 9×19mm Parabellum round is, after all, a pistol round, designed by Georg Luger at the very beginning of the 20th century. It still serves today, such is the value of the cartridge, but its principal application is for short-range combat only, even with the range extension that comes with a longer barrel. The 7.62×39mm cartridge, however, built upon German experiments conducted during World War II to provide optimum performance over almost all the *practical* combat ranges faced by soldiers in war, from 50m out to 400m. (Anything further than that would be engaged with sniper rifle and machine-gun fire.) The AK was simply the perfect package for that cartridge, and consequently the Soviet weapon became the giant of firearms history that it is today.

Although the Uzi was no longer standard military issue from the late 1960s, it was still used by many Israelis as a personal weapon. Here an Israeli settler in the West Bank during the 1980s carries an Uzi with a second magazine fixed to the one loaded into the pistol grip. (Getty Images)

Yet as any ordnance professional will tell you, no single firearm answers every need. In the right situations – such as fighting in bunkers and trenches on the Golan Heights – the Uzi proved that it could still be superior in very close-quarters combat. For covert operations in the hands of special forces, it was also the perfect fit for those wanting portable heavy firepower in an easily handled and concealed package. The Uzi therefore has filled – and continues to fill – a specific gap in the firearms mix of modern combatants.

So what of the Uzi's direct competitors in the SMG world – the MP5 and MAC-10? First we will look at a gun that in its time has garnered as much controversy as the Uzi, the MAC-10, designed by Gordon B. Ingram during the 1960s. To untrained eyes, the MAC-10 is often confused with an Uzi. Like the Uzi, the MAC-10 is a 9mm (or .45 ACP) telescoping bolt SMG that incorporates the magazine directly into the pistol grip. It features a basic wire extending stock, and its dimensions are in the same ballpark as the Mini Uzi – with its stock folded it measures just 269mm long. Weight is 2.84kg. Firing from a 32-shot magazine, the MAC-10 has a cyclical rate of fire of 1,090rpm, fast enough to cause serious alarm amongst legislators and police officers, and it has enough balance around the pistol grip to permit one-handed firing, should someone choose to do so. The barrel is threaded near the muzzle to take a suppressor if required, another feature that raised eyebrows. In fact, from the outset the gun was designed to mount a suppressor as part of the standard fitment, specifically a bulky two-stage device designed by Mitchell WerBell III of Sionics. This impressive piece of kit reduced what would normally be the loud ripping noise of firing down to a low-level popping, rivalled by the noise of the MAC-10's bolt ratcheting back and forth at great pace. The threaded muzzle, however,

could take a host of other fittings, including muzzle compensators and foregrips. Despite its visual similarity to the Uzi, the MAC-10 has a very different safety and fire selector arrangement. It does not feature the Uzi's grip safety; instead, it has a 'Safe' and 'Fire' switch located on the underside of the receiver. The fire selector switch is located separately on the left-hand side of the gun, with two options – 'Semi' and 'Full'.

The MAC-10 was developed for sale in the early 1970s by Military Armament Corporation (MAC), and two years after it entered the market MAC also brought out the MAC-11, which had even smaller overall dimensions and was chambered for the low-power .380 ACP, but with a rate of fire up to a racing 1,200rpm. MAC initially designed these weapons with military and law-enforcement markets in mind, and its official *Operating and Maintenance Manual* for the weapon illustrates how much it must have been seen as a competitor to the Uzi when it first emerged for sale:

> The Ingram Model 10 and Model 11 represent a significant breakthrough in compact submachine gun design. The M10 is available in 9mm Para and .45 ACP calibers, the M11 in .380 ACP caliber.

> Both Models are light in weight, [have] durable steel construction and [are] easy to fire, either semi-automatic or full automatic.

> The compact size of the M10 makes it especially suitable for tank crews, gun and mortar crews etc., and its selective fire capability makes it an excellent weapon for police use.

> The addition of a noise suppressor further enhances the performance, reducing the noise and eliminating muzzle flash.

> The weapon operates on the straight blowback principle and is magazine fed.

From this description, it is evident that the MAC-10 was looking to take a piece of the Uzi's market, yet in broad commercial terms the MAC-10 achieved nothing like the success of the Israeli weapon. Around 10,000 were manufactured for US Army and US police use, and a licence-built version was produced in Peru. In an age of expanding terrorism and assassinations, the MAC-10's suppressor selling point also began to look suspicious in the eyes of many governments, and export sales were limited. MAC actually went into bankruptcy in the 1970s, after which the MAC-10 was produced by a range of different companies, none of which managed to make the MAC-10 a commercial success. By 1986, MAC-10s were out of production.

The MAC-10's impact on the Uzi is not about stealing market share. What it represents are the increasing efforts of firearms manufacturers, starting in the 1970s, to take the Uzi layout and develop competing weapons, often with reduced dimensions and faster rates of fire. (The development of the Mini and Micro Uzi guns in the 1980s made sure that IMI stayed in the game.) To date, the list of Uzi-like firearms has grown substantially, and includes the Steyr TMP (Austria), FMK Mod 2 (Argentina), the ERO (Croatia – actually a direct Uzi copy), Socimi Type 821 (Italy), MGP-15 (Peru), BXP (South Africa), Sanna 77 (South Africa) and Star Z-84 (Spain). Increasingly, the Uzi found itself in a world of clone-like rivals, the similarities in layout making marketing the Uzi much more complicated, although the name stood out above the crowd.

While on the subject of Uzi-like competitors, one gun deserves a special mention. In 1994, the Sturm, Ruger company began production of an SMG known as the MP-9. What makes it fascinating for our study here is that it was developed by none other than Uziel Gal, during the 1980s. The basic layout suggests the influence of the original Uzi design, but the overall profile is distinguished by an openwork polymer frame that reaches out from the base of the pistol grip to the rear of the receiver, around which a new folding stock collapses in the folded position. Internally Gal opted for a closed bolt as standard to improve accuracy and fire control,

In the mid-1980s, San Jose Chief of Police Joseph McNamara holds up an Uzi Carbine (left) and a MAC-10, the latter fitted with a 32-round magazine. (© Roger Ressmeyer/Corbis)

An Israeli National Police Border Guard officer sights his Mini Uzi. Note how he aligns the front post with the target via the rear aperture; the cocking handle is also curved to prevent obscuring the sight picture. (Israel Weapon Industries)

and the Uzi's grip-activated safety is not present. Limited numbers of the MP-9 have been sold, but it gives an insight into the direction in which the Uzi might have evolved.

Going back to the MAC-10, this firearm might not have achieved commercial success, but it has regularly caught the headlines for criminal use. In fact, we might suggest that a problem for the Uzi is that it has frequently been tarred with the same brush as the MAC-10. Newspaper reports have frequently confused the two weapons, and often 'Uzi' is used as shorthand for any small, light, fast-firing SMG. Such lack of distinction is often unhelpful for separating fact from fiction regarding the non-legitimate use of the Uzi.

While the MAC-10 has had globally insignificant sales, at least to acceptable buyers, the same cannot be said of the Uzi's true competitor, the 9mm Heckler & Koch MP5. The MP5 represents a very different approach to SMG design, although the general layout follows quite traditional lines, with the magazine positioned in front of the trigger guard and the dimensions more akin to those of a carbine rifle. Internally, however, the MP5 uses a roller-delayed blowback system, derived from that of H&K's popular series of G3 rifles. In this system, bolt recoil is delayed via rollers attached to the bolt, these being forced out by the movement of the firing pin into recesses in the receiver wall as the bolt runs forward. When the gun is fired, the recoil has to force the rollers from the recesses to allow the bolt to recoil, hence imposing the requisite delay before the gun cycles through extraction, ejection and reloading. The action is very smooth and the rate of fire a controllable 500–600rpm. The MP5 also fires from a closed bolt as standard, which together with other sighting and ergonomic factors results in one of the most accurate SMGs available.

An interesting point to note is that a comparison of the MP5 and the standard Uzi shows the real success of Gal's original telescoping bolt design. The overall length of the standard MP5 in its stock-folded configuration is 550mm, and the total barrel length is 255mm. The Uzi, by contrast, has a stock-folded length of 470mm – a full 80mm shorter than the MP5 – but at 260mm its barrel length actually exceeds that of the German gun.

The MP5 is an exceptionally high-quality gun, expensive to make and buy, and a broad range of variants have been created to suit all tastes in the special forces and law-enforcement communities. Sales have been extremely high, to more than 50 export markets and with licensed producers in Greece, Iran, Mexico, Pakistan, Saudi Arabia, Sudan, Turkey and the UK. Almost every major counter-terrorist and SWAT-style law-enforcement unit worldwide has adopted the MP5, for reasons explained by special operations expert Leroy Thompson:

Highly controllable, compact, accurate, able to carry various specialised sighting devices and firing a pistol round which will not risk over-penetration and endanger hostages as much as a rifle round would, the MP-5 is an outstanding hostage rescue weapon. Because of its shoulder stock and pistol grip, the MP-5 offers a more stable shooting platform for precision shot placement ... Some H&K MP-5s are fitted with a three-round burst setting on the selector switch ... The versatility of the MP-5 also makes it highly desirable among HRUs [hostage-rescue units].[16]

US Army soldiers train with the MP5, the most successful SMG type in terms of special forces and law-enforcement use since the 1970s. Its carbine-like layout and closed-bolt configuration make it especially accurate. (US Department of Defense)

The first sentence of this quotation lists characteristics present in the Uzi, but the MP5's inclusion of more substantial furniture, its three-round burst facility (on some models) and the sheer range of variants set it apart somewhat from its rivals. Variant MP5s include a dedicated suppressed version, the MP5SD, various folding-stock guns and a cut-down type, the MP5K, which also features a front grip to provide a very stable platform. (Note, though, that Uzis can also be fitted with aftermarket front grips if desired.)

The MP5 carries almost no criminal connotations (except in a handful of films), and its televised use by the SAS in their breaking of the Iranian Embassy siege in London in 1980 secured its reputation as a high-end special ops weapon. Its impact on sales of the Uzi has been profound, but it doesn't answer every need in the market. On account of its high cost, the MP5 has been unsuited for adoption on a large scale by military forces.

[16] Leroy Thompson, *Hostage Rescue Manual*, London: Greenhill (2001)

In fact, the Bundeswehr stuck with the Uzi over their native MP5 largely because of cost, but also because the Uzi perfectly answered their needs within their budget. More specialist units such as the *Grenzschutzgruppe 9* (GSG 9; Border Guard Group 9) counter-terrorist force, however, opted for the MP5.

What the Uzi has achieved which the MP5 has not is that it has been carried in major wars as a standard weapon of an army. If anything, the Uzi's impact is more similar to that of the AK-47, in that it has appeared around the entire world in every conceivable type of conflict, from terrorism in Northern Ireland to civil wars in Africa and tank battles in the Sinai desert. Few weapons can claim such broad authority or distribution.

Perhaps more than any other weapon, the Uzi also became an icon of the IDF, and of Israel's military independence. In an interview for the Fox News Channel in 2003, Yitfah Shapir of the Jaffee Center for Strategic Studies at Tel Aviv University, a former IDF soldier, noted nostalgically: 'It was the first Israeli weapon after 2,000 years of diaspora … I can still disassemble an Uzi with my eyes closed, hands tied behind my back, even if you wake me in the middle of the night' (AP, 17 December 2003). Israel is a country that has experienced more warfare than almost any other post-war nation. Only a gun that soldiers could trust with their lives would have become so enduring.

A Micro Uzi fitted with a large suppressor. Combined with the low-velocity 9mm round, such devices significantly reduce the audible noise of firing. This weapon also has a front grip and a Mepro 21 reflex sight. (Israel Weapon Industries)

CONCLUSION

In October 2008, eight-year-old Christopher Bizilj of Ashford, Connecticut, was attending the Machine Gun Shoot and Firearms Expo at the Westfield Sportsman's Club, also in Connecticut, where he had the chance to shoot a Mini Uzi on full-auto. Despite being under adult supervision throughout, the boy lost control of the recoil while firing a burst. The muzzle kicked upwards and back while the boy still kept his finger on the trigger, resulting in Christopher being struck in the head by a 9mm round. He was pronounced dead in hospital shortly afterwards.

At the time of writing, the court case is playing out in front of the world's media, raising broad issues around the relationship children have with firearms, and around the safe handling of full-auto weapons by the public. The Uzi itself is in the news again, for all the wrong reasons.

What the sad case of Christopher Bizilj reminds us that is that the Uzi, even in its semi-auto forms, is a military-grade weapon that like all firearms must be handled with respect. It was born for the battlefield, and commands responsibility in its use, especially as the production of new versions and the durability of older weapons mean that it will probably be around for many decades to come.

For the IDF, however, the Uzi's chapter has recently come to an end. In 2003, 50 years after the gun first came into service, the Uzi was withdrawn from all military service, including its use as a training weapon, although it doubtless remains as a option for elite units. The very next year a new weapon was selected by the IDF as its future standard assault rifle. The Tavor, also developed by IMI, is a 5.56×45mm NATO gas-operated, rotating-bolt rifle designed around the bullpup layout used in weapons such as the British SA80. Bullpup firearms position the bolt carrier group and magazine behind the pistol grip, the result being that the rifle can be the manageable length of a carbine but retain the full barrel length of a rifle. For example, the conventionally structured M16A2 rifle has an overall length of

An Israeli soldier guards an Arab prisoner in the West Bank territory during the Six-Day War, carrying an early wooden-stocked Uzi. The weapon's compact dimensions made it ideally suited to use aboard vehicles. (Pierre Guillaud/AFP/Getty Images.

1,006mm and a barrel length of 508mm. The standard Tavor TAR-21 model has an overall length of just 720mm, but still manages to keep its barrel length a respectable 460mm. For special forces personnel who need something more portable, a shorter version called the CTAR is available, while the Tavor family also includes bipod-mounted sharpshooter versions and types configured to hold under-barrel grenade launchers. Unlike the Uzi, its centre of gravity is nearly in the soldier's shoulder, not over the pistol grip, so it makes the rapid acquisition of targets a fluid and instinctive action. Combined with the use of ultra-modern ergonomics in its design, it makes the traditional Uzi appear very antiquated.

More and more countries that retain the Uzi are likely to phase them out in the near future. Just as new generations of assault rifle appear, the rise of the personal defence weapon (PDW) is also chipping into remaining stocks of the Uzi. The PDW is much like a post-war era SMG, being a compact semi- or full-auto firearm designed principally for use by vehicle crews and special forces soldiers. Unlike the SMG, the PDW tends to fire heavier, more powerful rounds with improved range performance and the capability to penetrate some forms of body armour. Recent examples include the FN P90, a bizarre-looking fully ambidextrous bullpup weapon firing a powerful 5.7×28mm round at 715m/sec. Similarly, the German Bundeswehr and GSG 9 are now adopting the H&K MP7, which like the Uzi has the magazine within the pistol grip, but instead fires a 4.6×30mm round at similar velocities to the P90.

The rise of the PDW, alongside new versions of carbines and assault rifles, will probably mean that many Uzis are ousted from military use over the next few decades. Yet we should never underestimate the Uzi design. The reason why the Uzi has endured in service for such a long period of history is the fundamental integrity of its design. Furthermore, that design has been tested to its limits in combat, and rarely been found wanting if used within the parameters for which it was created. Even weapons made during the 1960s are still in circulation around the world, and with proper maintenance and the occasional replacement of key parts they should stay operational for many years to come. Of the thousands of firearms developed since the end of World War II, few can rival the Uzi's undeniable reputation.

This Micro Uzi is fitted with a Mepro 21 Reflex Sight, designed to provide rapid aiming in all light conditions, without the need for battery power. Illumination of the aiming point is provided by a fibre-optic collector system during the day, and by a miniature self-powered tritium light source at night. (Israel Weapon Industries)

GLOSSARY

ACP: Automatic Colt Pistol (cartridge)

BLOWBACK: A system of firearms operation that uses the breech pressure generated upon firing to operate the bolt

BOLT: The part of a firearm that closes the breech of the firearm and often performs the functions of loading, extraction and (via a firing pin) ignition

BREECH-BLOCK: A mechanism designed to close the breech for firing; roughly analogous to 'bolt' (*q.v.*)

BREECH: The rear end of a gun barrel

CARBINE: A shortened rifle

CHAMBER: The section at the rear of the barrel into which the cartridge is seated for firing

CLOSED BOLT: Refers to firearms in which the bolt/breech-block is closed up to the chamber before the trigger is pulled

COOK-OFF: The involuntary discharge of a cartridge by the build-up of heat in the chamber from firing

EJECTOR: The mechanism that throws an empty cartridge case clear of a gun following extraction from the chamber

EXTRACTOR: The mechanism that removes an empty cartridge case from the chamber after firing

GAS OPERATION: A system of operating the cycle of a firearm using gas tapped off from burning propellant

LOCK TIME: The time interval between pulling the trigger and the gun firing

OPEN BOLT: Refers to firearms in which the bolt/breech-block is held back from the breech before the trigger is pulled

RECEIVER: The main outer body of a gun, which holds the firearm's action

SEMI-AUTOMATIC: A weapon that fires one round and reloads ready for firing with every pull of the trigger

SUPPRESSOR: Device to reduce the audible sound of firing

BIBLIOGRAPHY

Allsop, D.F., and M.A. Toomey, *Small Arms*, Brassey's Land Warfare vol. 6, London: Brassey's, 1999

Bowen, Jeremy, *Six Days: How the 1967 War Shaped the Middle East*, London: Simon & Schuster, 2003

Chivers, C.J., *The Gun: The AK47 and the Evolution of War*, London: Penguin, 2004

Geller, Doron, 'Operation Spring of Youth', The Pedagogic Center, The Department for Jewish Zionist Education, The Jewish Agency for Israel (1992–2005): <http://www.jewishvirtuallibrary.org/jsource/History/opspring.html>

Hammel, Eric, *Six Days in June: How Israel won the 1967 Arab-Israeli War*, New York, NY: Scribner's, 1992

Hogg, Ian, *Israeli War Machine: The Men; The Machines; The Tactics*, London: Quarto, 1983

Hogg, Ian, and John Weeks, *Military Small Arms of the 20th Century*, London: Arms and Armour Press, 1991

Israel Military Industries Ltd, *Uzi 9mm Submachine Gun: Instruction Manual*, Ramat Hasharon: IWI (n.d.)

Israel Weapon Industries Ltd, *Micro Uzi Armorer Course: Instructor's Manual Manual*, Ramat Hasharon: IWI (n.d.)

Katz, Samuel, *The Illustrated Guide to the World's Top Counter-Terrorist Forces*, Hong Kong: Concord, 1995

Katz, Samuel, *Israeli Elite Units Since 1948*, Oxford: Osprey, 1988

Korwin, Alan, *Gun Laws of America*, Phoenix, AZ: Bloomfield Press, 2003

McNab, Chris, *Deadly Force: Firearms and American Law Enforcement*, Oxford: Osprey, 2009

McNab, Chris, and Hunter Keeter, *Tools of Violence: Guns, Tanks and Dirty Bombs*, Oxford: Osprey, 2008

n.a., *Uzi SMG: Operation Manual*, El Dorado, AR: Desert Publications, 1983

TAAS – Israel Industries Ltd, *Mini Uzi 9mm Submachine Gun: Instruction Manual*, Ramat Hasharon: IWI (n.d.)

Thompson, Leroy, *Hostage Rescue Manual*, London: Greenhill, 2001

INDEX

References to illustrations are shown in **bold**.